BACK YOURSELF

BACK YOURSELF

A Wellbeing Guide to Healing from Racial Trauma

LILDONIA LAWRENCE

Published in 2025 by Trigger Publishing
An imprint of Shaw Callaghan Ltd

UK Office
The Stanley Building
7 Pancras Square
Kings Cross
London N1C 4AG

US Office
On Point Executive Center, Inc
3030 N Rocky Point Drive W
Suite 150
Tampa, FL 33607
www.triggerpublishing.com

Text © 2025 Lildonia Lawrence
Design and layout © 2025 Shaw Callaghan Ltd

Lildonia Lawrence has asserted her moral right to be identified as the author of this Work in accordance with the Copyright Designs and Patents Act 1988.

All rights reserved. No part of this publication may be reproduced, stored in a retrieval system, or transmitted in any form or by any means, electronically, mechanical, photocopying, recording or otherwise, without the prior permission of the copyright owners and the publishers.

A CIP catalogue record for this book is available upon request from the British Library
ISBN: 978-1-83796-089-7
eBook ISBN: 978-1-83796-090-3

Cover design by Francesca Corsini
Typeset by Lapiz Digital Services

Trigger Publishing encourages diversity and different viewpoints. However, all views, thoughts and opinions expressed in this book are the author's own and are not necessarily representative of us as an organization.

All material in this book is set out in good faith for general guidance and no liability can be accepted for loss or expense incurred in following the information given. In particular this book is not intended to replace expert medical or psychiatric advice. It is intended for informational purposes only and for your own personal use and guidance. It is not intended to act as a substitute for professional medical advice. The author is not a medical practitioner nor a counsellor, and professional advice should be sought if desired before embarking on any health-related programme.

TABLE OF CONTENTS

Prologue	vii
Introduction	1

1 **Managing Microaggressions:** The impact of microaggressions 7
2 **Overcoming Othering:** What does it mean to be the other? 31
3 **Combatting Cultural Conflict:** The impact of a split identity 65
4 **Coping with Colourism:** The history of colourism 87
5 **Transforming Transgenerational Trauma:** Signs and symptoms of secondary trauma 115

Afterword	145
Acknowledgements	149
Glossary	151
Additional Resources	155
References	159

PROLOGUE

"I don't know what she's moaning about. It's not as if I called her a c**t or a n***er."

These were the words spat at my swim teacher by a group of racist thugs as she attempted to advocate for me in the face of their racism. On that morning, just a short while ago, I sat in the sauna, as I do every Monday. Every week I found myself surrounded by a gang of bigoted and aggressive thugs. Each time I would hear them cackling with laughter as they made fun of anyone they perceived as "different": the Muslim women in their modest wear, the queer gym instructor, and the newly arrived refugee communities accessing the pool.

They were vile, and the weight of their words weighed heavy on me every single week, but I refused to stop accessing my local leisure centre. So, I took up my rightful space in the sauna week after week, crammed in the corner trying my best to avoid these big-mouthed bigots.

On this particular day, there were more than usual: eight men and two women. I was vastly outnumbered and for whatever reason they chose that day to attack me verbally. As I sat there minding my business, they made jokes about the "tanned" skin complexion of one of the group members. He'd been on holiday and "was as dark as a ...".

Their words cut through the air like knives, and with every jibe, the cuts dug deeper into my being. They thought they were so hilarious as they bantered to one another, calling me "dipped with the coal tar brush", an antiquated racial slur to describe someone who appears to have mixed African heritage.

This time, though, I had had enough. I confronted them, then and there in the sauna. In the pitch black, in my swimming costume with no allies in sight. My voice trembled and my heart pounded, yet I told them exactly what I thought of their bullying and discrimination.

They didn't listen. Of course they didn't. They sneered and laughed, and they taunted me as my eyes spilt over with tears. Their hatred and dismissal were a bitter reminder of the deep-seated racism that still permeates our world.

This ordeal was one of the most racially traumatic that I've endured. At the time, the cacophony of emotions was overwhelming. I felt anger, humiliation, powerlessness and fear. I was disappointed in the two women who witnessed but didn't intervene. I felt disgusted at the threats they threw at my swimming teacher, who ran in to help when I fled the sauna in tears.

I couldn't believe that during the process of writing a book on racial healing, I experienced a vicious racist incident. One thing that I'll always hold near to my heart is that despite the anger and fear, I was able to speak up for myself in that moment. My voice, as wobbly as it may have been, was heard. Not only in that moment in the sauna, but also in my police statement and in my complaint to the leisure centre.

PROLOGUE

It definitely wasn't easy to speak up for myself, but when I came out the other side, it reminded me of the power of my voice, the strength of my convictions and the importance of my work.

It was this encounter that bolstered my conviction in the creation of this book, this experience that reminded me of the impact of racism on wellbeing and the vital importance of wellbeing resources for us and by us.

INTRODUCTION

Dearest reader, thank you so much for being here. This book has been a long time in the making, and the fact that you have picked it up means the world to me!

This project is the culmination of years of work in the form of one-to-one sessions, group coaching, training and workshops with culturally diverse people, interspersed with my own experience of being a woman of colour.

So, who am I? Well, my name is Lildonia Lawrence, and I am a half-Alaskan, half-Bajan, British-born, mixed-heritage Black woman. I am a second-generation immigrant and proud of it! I have been working as a mental health and wellbeing coach since 2010, and my big passion is helping people to improve their physical, emotional and spiritual health, as well as their mental health and wellbeing. I am somewhat fanatical about my global-majority community and spend a lot of time working to support positive wellbeing across the diaspora.

During my years in the field, I noticed patterns coming up with clients of colour living as a racialized minority in majority-white environments, meaning they're part of the 85 per cent of the planet's population who are of Indigenous, African, Asian or Latin American descent. Alongside the everyday worries and woes, there were particularly nuanced issues coming up for my Black and brown client base.

People from cultural backgrounds that had seemingly little in common were bringing very similar topics to the sessions: their experiences of microaggressions, feelings of being on the outside and battles with colourism, and the transmission of cultural trauma. I followed these threads of connection, and during my reflective practice, I began taking note of these themes.

As these seeds of potential began to grow in my mind, I decided to take a leap of faith and plant them. Those seedlings eventually grew into this book ... a wellbeing guide for culturally diverse humans! It's a resource for exploring and gently counselling my fellow people of colour in the areas of wellbeing that are typically impacted by our race, culture, faith or ethnicity.

WHO IS THIS BOOK FOR?

If you are reading this book, then it is for you! This book is for anyone who has experienced racism or racial trauma. You'll notice I use different terms like **Black, Indigenous and people of colour** (BIPOC), **people of colour** (POC), **racialized individuals**, **melanated** and **global majority** fairly interchangeably. I vary usage depending on the context and to honour the fact that we all identify differently.

It's important to understand that these terms aren't just about race – they can also include people from various ethno-religious and pan-ethnic backgrounds. For example, members of the Jewish Diaspora or Roma

INTRODUCTION

and Traveller communities may share these experiences, even if they don't necessarily identify as people of colour. The concept of "race" is ever evolving, and it is important for us to honour the lived experience of all groups who may experience racial discrimination based on their ethnicity, or who do not fall under the umbrella of Western "whiteness". By using these different terms, I aim to be inclusive and respectful of the diversity within our community.

As a global-majority community, we are not a monolith, and so it is impossible to find language that resonates with everyone. Language is rapidly evolving and the words we use to describe our identity are extremely personal, so please feel free to mentally swap out terms that do not resonate. I am not the identity police, and for me, however you identify is how I will be blessed to accept you!

And for our white brothers and sisters who have ended up here – welcome. Alongside my work as a BIPOC wellbeing specialist, much of my time is spent supporting allies who are on a journey of becoming (and being) anti-racist. This book is for you, for those of you who are trying to do the often difficult (but extremely worthwhile) job of being an ally to our communities.

My hope is that through reading these words, you will get an in-depth understanding of the historical context of racism and racial discrimination, along with a deeper insight into the global-majority communities' lived experience. Please read this book with an open mind and heart in support of your non-white colleagues, friends and family members. You have more power to change "The System" than we ever will, and so it is up to you to create change from within.

HOW THIS BOOK WILL HELP YOU

My deepest wish for you, reader, is that my words support you on your journey to and through holistic wellbeing. Navigating the often complex experience of being a person of colour in majority-white spaces can be challenging. There is a lot of talk about anti-oppressive and anti-racist practice (which is wonderful!), but there is little support for the people who are still marginalized and oppressed under these systems.

That is where this book comes in! It is your friendly, pocket-sized guide to all things wellbeing in a melanated body. In each chapter, I will cover a topic that I have seen come up in my BIPOC-specific wellbeing sessions. Each chapter includes stories from my lived experience, as well as case studies and tools you can use straight away.

These are meaty topics, and at times, doing this self-care and reflective work can be overwhelming. Please ensure you look after yourself – choose reading time where you will not be disturbed and allow yourself all the self-care you need.

HOW TO USE THIS BOOK

This book is designed to be read in chronological order. Each chapter covers a historical and social context, along with top tips, reflective exercises, and tools to support healing in mind, body and spirit. Feel free to highlight, bend page corners or bookmark – this is designed to be a work-along manual that you can come back to time and time again.

INTRODUCTION

> ## A NOTE ON CASE STUDIES
>
> Throughout the book, you will see case studies inspired by clients I have worked with in the past. All are rooted in real-life experiences and aim to illustrate concepts and themes. However, all identifying information – names, locations and distinctive features – have been meticulously removed or altered to ensure the privacy and confidentiality of those involved.
>
> The purpose of these case studies is purely educational, and any resemblance to actual persons, living or deceased, or to real events, is purely coincidental.

I hope that by the end of this book you will have a deeper understanding of yourself, your roots, and the skills you possess that will help you to BACK YOURSELF!

And with all that being said … let's get started!

1

MANAGING MICROAGGRESSIONS

THE IMPACT OF MICROAGGRESSIONS

It was 2017. I was travelling in Canada, newly single and getting acquainted with the world of dating apps. I sat in the living room of a long-time friend as I swiped like a kid in a candy store – I had way too much choice. My friend, of Russian heritage, asked to see my phone wanting to see what kind of folks I was into.

It so happened that my last three matches were with an Ethiopian man, an Indo-Caribbean woman and an Italian-American guy. My friend seemed impressed by my expansive and global approach to dating. "I thought you'd only match with Black guys, Lil! But I guess you're so well spoken and educated that you can attract any race."

My words caught in my throat at that moment. I didn't know what to say. Her insinuation was that my level of education somehow made me a "suitable candidate" for white men. I was shocked, hurt and offended, but I didn't feel I could say anything in response. I was on vacation, I was in my friend's house and I felt vulnerable.

My pal was a person who would be shocked to be deemed as a racist – she was, in fact, in a relationship with a Black man – but that didn't stop the microaggressions from pouring out from her subconscious.

Microaggressive behaviour is one of the most frequently discussed topics in my health and wellbeing sessions with people of colour. My experience with my friend was the perfect example of a comment said in passing meant very little to the perpetrator, but was absolutely crushing for the recipient. I doubt my friend even remembers this incident, but for me, it was something I'll never forget. These everyday slights, slurs or comments are always offensive and are anything but micro.

Microaggressions are the bane of many racialized people's existence, and the impact they have is tremendous. They're not always verbalized directly – sometimes they're simply implied and sometimes they're conveyed through body language or action – but they're *always* directed toward marginalized or minority groups.

Whether they're aware of it or not, people of colour, women, members of the LGBTQIA+ community, those with disabilities, and ethnic or religious minorities experience microaggressions frequently. They can come from people we know, from the mass media or even from strangers on the street.

Microaggressions are painful. They're often covert, and they are part and parcel of our daily experience, two aspects that make them difficult to call out. They can show up in many ways, and sometimes we don't even realize we've been a target of microaggressions until after the event (sometimes days, weeks or even months later).

The most common one we as people of colour tend to deal with is having someone ask us to confirm or validate our ethnic or cultural origin. It's the dreaded, "But where are you *really* from?" follow-up question, which signifies that there's disbelief when you say you're British, American, Canadian, French, etc. But it's also being told you don't seem or speak or act like your race or ethnicity. It's the presumption about what music you're into, what food you eat or what your family dynamic is like, all based on the colour of your skin, the ancestry you possess or your country of origin.

A 2021 study found that a massive 67 per cent of people report experiencing microaggressions at work, with 22 per cent experiencing microaggressions several times within a week. Out of those who took part in this study, 71 per cent felt their experiences were due to their gender, and 38 per cent believed it was due to their race and/or ancestry, highlighting the double discrimination impact of gender and race (Farid et al.).

I remember one time at work, while getting ready for the Christmas night out, an older female colleague commented on my tiny waist and "classic big Black girl's butt". I was mortified, but despite my obvious shock, she proceeded to tell me how much her daughters love the "Black girl butt", and how jealous they would have been if they had seen me.

This happened while I was working at a disability awareness charity! You would think staff there would be aware of damaging or discriminatory language, but the thing is, people are often only cognizant of prejudices in the areas that affect them. Sometimes, as humans, we display egocentric bias, a type of cognition that causes us to centre ourselves and focus on our own perspective. This means that we can often unknowingly overlook the lived experience of others. For example, a white disabled woman may be aware of sexism and ableism, but lack of awareness of the lived experience of racism. A straight, cis-gendered man of colour may have an awareness of racism and xenophobia, but little understanding of the experiences of women or the queer community.

We can all display an egocentric bias – in some ways this is normal and natural. However, it is important for us to challenge our internal thought processes and learn more about others so that we can work toward greater understanding of those different to ourselves.

CASE STUDY: Microaggressions in the workplace

Michael is a 28-year-old man of Ugandan heritage. He was born in Uganda and adopted by a Scottish mother and Italian father when he was five years old. Michael spent his early years in Italy and moved to the UK to study at university.

Shortly after his 28th birthday, Michael got a job in a multinational corporation. On his first day, he was introduced to the Italian team. When Michael told the team that he was Italian, the manager responded stating that it was lovely to see someone who was "sort of Italian" in the team.

▲ Despite only ever referring to himself as Italian, the manager continually referred to him as "half", "sort of" and "kind of" Italian. Subconsciously, his manager was signalling that regardless of how Michael identified, he did not perceive him as Italian because of his skin colour. This subtly eroded Michael's sense of self and his confidence in connecting with the wider team.

It's not only within work contexts that microaggressions show up – they also present in education, healthcare and even within our own families and friends. Having a partner, child or best friend of colour does not make you immune from displaying microaggressions. Even *being* a person of colour doesn't exempt you – we've got a lot of work to do within our communities. There is still a lot of racism toward racialized people even within diverse ethnic and cultural communities, such as anti-Blackness (more on this later!).

I recall a time when I was sitting on a platform waiting for the train. A giggling group of women on a hen-do asked me to take a picture of them and, of course, I happily obliged. It was an all-white group, except for a light-skinned Black woman with a beautiful, curly, coiled head of hair. The group snuggled in for their shot, and as they did, an older lady at the back dodged and squirmed as she tried to hide from view. The bride turned to her and raucously shouted, "You don't need to hide behind her, her hair isn't that big," all the while patting her brown friend's head like some sort of stray dog. The rest of the group cried with laughter while the poor lady visibly flinched.

I would have never intervened in a conversation between this friendship group, but a massive part of me wanted to grab this afro-haired queen and take her out for a nice meal, just to get her away from the barrage of microaggressions. Now, undoubtedly this woman had an intimate connection with the bride, but it still didn't stop those comments. This group could have been the best of friends, but they still found it acceptable to make fun of their companion due to a feature of her ethnic background. The subtext of a microaggression is that the recipient is seen as lesser than, and in this instance, the lady who commented revealed her unconscious belief that the Black body is open for ridicule.

Most people would be horrified to think that they perpetuate microaggressions, but unfortunately, every single one of us holds unconscious biases beneath the surface. Project Implicit, a well-known study carried out by Harvard University, consistently reported that a high number of participants showed a preference for white people over Black people, and as a result, tended to be unfriendlier toward them even when they self-reported liberal and egalitarian points of view (Greenwald et al.). These biases can cause people to act in ways that are discriminatory, whether that is their conscious intention or not.

Something that plays into this is implicit associations – the mental associations that people make between different concepts. I remember speaking with a colleague who had recently moved to London from Cornwall. He described feeling mortified that his housemate had pointed out to him that he crossed the street every time he saw a group of Black men. My colleague had realized that he had unwittingly absorbed associations and stereotypes about Black men being dangerous.

This stereotype is something that is confessed to me often by white people in my anti-racism sessions. There is an unconscious belief in our society that Black men are dangerous. It is unconscious belief systems like this that can manifest in daily interactions in the form of microaggressions and prejudiced speech or action.

When speaking with the Black men in my life, I can see how this has impacted them. For example, my father would consistently jog at 5am to avoid being seen and not "scare" people. And a friend of mine would always hide if his girlfriend's father came around because "no French man wants to find a Black man in his daughter's bed". Events such as these can cause Black men to lose their self-esteem, lack confidence and internalize negative messaging about themselves and others like them. It's a vicious cycle of bias, implicit association and a negative impact on the recipients of that bias.

Being on the receiving end of microaggressions can be extremely painful and degrading. They are harmful, and despite the name, they are anything but micro – the impact they have over time is great and can severely impact a person's mental health. Being constantly told you're not good enough, even if it's indirectly, can have a massive impact on self-esteem and self-worth.

At times, I've been shocked by the microaggressions that have passed the lips of people I care about, respect and trust, and this has made me feel like nowhere is safe. I remember a particular experience when I attended an event with my ex-partner, who was of mixed heritage: white British and Black Caribbean. He and I were the only people of colour at the event.

BACK YOURSELF

I had a constant stream of people asking me where I was from. The worst was a drunken man telling me about his recent Caribbean cruise and asking what I thought about the fact that Caribbean men "all have loads of kids". I found the comments offensive and stereotypical, and I couldn't believe these conversations were being openly had.

Years later, when I watched director Jordan Peele's acclaimed film *Get Out*, I resonated with the main character, Chris, a young African American who ends up bamboozled, trapped and racially pursued by his white girlfriend's family. Just as they're depicted in the film, these experiences can feel like they've happened while we're under hypnosis, as they can be so covert and hard to fully identify. At the time of the event I attended with my ex-partner, I was in my early twenties and grossly outnumbered, and I certainly didn't feel comfortable to challenge any of the comments. In fact, as a young person finding my feet, I found it hard enough to speak up for myself in general, let alone surrounding the murky topics of race and identity. When speaking to friends younger than myself, I note a sense of imposter syndrome, a feeling of not being established enough to challenge authority, those older than us and the status quo. If I could talk to my 20-year-old self now, I'd let her know that there are no qualifications needed to speak up for yourself, and that if something feels off, it usually is.

Despite there being more discussions about race and equity than ever, we still have a long way to go, and it can be really difficult to challenge microaggressions, especially when you are the only person of colour in an all-white space. In my grandparents' and great-grandparents' generations, there was a strongly rooted acceptance that "white [was] right" – that the white man's word was the law. As sad as that is, it's not surprising based on the experiences they would have had with colonization, the transatlantic slave trade and mass migration. These days, I feel much more comfortable discussing issues of race and identity, but I still find it difficult to call someone out when they've said something inappropriate. It's particularly difficult in an all-white space or when engaging with those who have little to no knowledge of anti-racism work. This is why practice, patience and a big dose of compassion are needed in our journeys of self-advocacy.

The beliefs that lend themselves to microaggressions didn't come about by accident – they were a key component of the West's strategy to conquer. White colonizers used a combination of indoctrination and force to push the narrative that white people were superior to other races. The main issue with the enduring belief in whiteness as the "superior" race is that it is intrinsically flawed. Race is not a biological reality, but a social construct. There are very few genetic or biological differences between races. During the inception of colonization, European colonialists created the concept of race, describing a racial hierarchy with white people at the top and Black people at the bottom. Prior to that, the concept of race did not exist at all.

This racial hierarchy was developed to take hold of territory, subordinate melanated bodies and gain control. This model gained popularity during the 18th and 19th centuries and was falsely documented within religious charters to incorrectly evidence that by divine and God-given design, Caucasian (white) people were a superior race. Books such as *Racial Formation in the United States* speak about the creation of race as a social construct, highlighting its dynamic nature shaped by history and politics, as opposed to biological fact (Omi & Winant).

So, as we can see, there *is* no superior race! Despite this glaringly obvious fact, these methods were used as early as the 1400s to justify the colonization, enslavement and dehumanization of Indigenous Africans, Americans and Asians, and other non-Christian people. Both white and non-white people have absorbed this messaging for hundreds of years, both consciously and unconsciously. Couple this with systemic structures of oppression, and we have a perfect storm for a discriminatory and biased society.

It's no wonder that at times we feel unworthy – we've had centuries of being told that the bodies we exist in are not worthy. But spoiler alert, my friends: white is *not* always right, and we need to work toward changing cultural patterns. We must start believing that we too have the right to be in our power, speak our truths and exist as our authentic and amazing selves.

ADVOCATING FOR YOURSELF

At the start of this book, I shared my experience of racism at the swimming pool. It was a very fear-inducing experience and ultimately stopped me from using that leisure centre.

To be clear, what I experienced was more than a microaggression, but the emotional impact of racism, whether micro or macro, is still huge. In my case, the emotional toll on me was great, and I thought about backing down, but with the help of a few key supporters in my life, I found the strength to report the incident to the police, put in an official complaint and gain assistance from a race-hate charity.

Standing your ground in the face of discrimination can be enormously challenging. Before standing up for yourself, you must first recognize that you are experiencing a microaggression, and that alone can be tough.

The best piece of advice I can give in this area is to trust your gut – if something feels off, then it usually is. People of colour have had many years of being told that the experiences they report are fabrications. Tune into your body, listen to your intuition and trust yourself!

Another key to dealing with microaggressions is having strong boundaries and being assertive. It's not always easy, and it can be intimidating and uncomfortable, but advocating for yourself is a way to protect your peace and become empowered.

Since the resurgence of the Black Lives Matter movement in 2020, equality, diversity and inclusion have been on top of the agenda for countless individuals and organizations. This has given us more of a platform than ever to highlight injustice and create room for change. I know I wouldn't have felt as comfortable calling out microaggressions even five years ago, but now that the social justice landscape has changed, I feel much more at ease raising concerns.

A big part of advocating for yourself is having an awareness of your own boundaries. Boundaries are very subjective and vary from one person to another, but maintaining personal boundaries is vital for feeling a sense of safety, security and wellbeing.

Our boundaries differ in different environments, and our ability to maintain them varies, too. When we have permeable boundaries, we can end up accepting behaviour that we are unhappy with, staying quiet when we want to speak up or saying yes when we want to say no. Conversely, having inflexible boundaries means being unmoving or unyielding with your personal preferences and limitations. Generally, we are aiming for somewhere in the middle: holding assertive boundaries while respecting those around us. However, in the face of inequity, there will be times when you must be unmoving and resolute in your belief systems.

A particular example that comes to mind is when an acquaintance (demographic white straight male) would continually challenge me on social media whenever I posted about homophobia or racism. He would write poorly worded paragraphs stating that I was wrong, and that xenophobia, homophobia and racial prejudice did not exist in the UK. After a few incidents of back-and-forth direct messaging, I decided that he wasn't worth my time, so I blocked him! You are allowed not to accept behaviour you find objectionable – you are allowed to say no, and you are allowed to call someone out if they are disrespectful.

When you experience a microaggression, a range of emotions can flow through you: shock, anger, embarrassment, sadness and shame, to name a few. When this happens, if possible, take a moment to collect your thoughts and take a deep breath before responding. You don't need to apologize for feeling offended, you don't need to give intricate reasoning for why the behaviour was unacceptable, and you do not need to pretend to be okay with it if you're not.

> **TOP TIP:** Have your responses ready
>
> Memorize some phrases you can use in the face of microaggressions, such as:
>
> 1. "I don't find that funny."
> 2. "That is not an acceptable comment."
> 3. "What you just said was offensive."
> 4. "I find your words/behaviour inappropriate."
> 5. "Please refrain from making offensive comments about …"

To clarify, not everyone who perpetrates harm through microaggressive speech is a bad person. Sometimes, people are simply ignorant, unaware of the harm they are causing and/or deeply unconscious.

Below are two real-life examples of unacceptable behaviour I've had to deal with, one with someone I knew, liked and trusted, and the other with a stranger.

TEXT CONVERSATION BETWEEN AN EX-COLLEAGUE AND I

Colleague: Hey Lildonia, are you still delivering anti-racism training?
Me: Hey! I am. What's it regarding?
Colleague: My work is looking for a volunteer to deliver anti-racism training at their equality and diversity conference.
Me: Thanks for checking in. I'd be happy to discuss the possibility of paid delivery for your organization. However, I don't do any voluntary anti-racism training, as it perpetuates the cycle of unpaid labour for Black

and brown people. This is the exact upholding of capitalism and white supremacy that I'm working to dismantle.
Colleague: Fair enough! I completely agree. I think it is bad that they're even asking – I'll give them feedback and see what I can do!

In this scenario, I initially felt quite awkward because I liked and respected the person who asked the question. However, if I did not express my objection, I would have ended up feeling pushed into delivering the session, or my colleague could have assumed that I was comfortable with requests like this. It's not always easy, but our voices and opinions must be heard. We no longer need to downplay situations that occur, particularly in the workplace where we have legislation and policy designed to support us.

CONVERSATION WITH AN EVENTS COORDINATOR

Events coordinator: Okay, so what type of catering will you require for the event?
Me: I'm half Caribbean, so ideally, I'd like a Caribbean theme.
Events coordinator: Lovely! I can just smell the jerk chicken now. I'm sure our chefs can knock up a Jamaican-themed menu.
Me: I actually don't eat meat, plus I'm not Jamaican. I'm from Barbados.
Events coordinator, blushing and clearly mortified: I'm so sorry, I got a bit carried away there.
Me: That's okay, thanks for apologizing.

In the second situation, I was confronting a stranger. It would have been easy to let it go, but I probably would have regretted not calling out their obvious conflation of Caribbean culture and countries. This particular person was extremely apologetic, so I was able to forgive the error and move on. It gave me a good chance to practise my boundaries and it was a moment of learning for the events coordinator.

Just like the elders in our community, we too have been programmed with certain beliefs, and it is important that we reflect on our upbringing and what we've been taught about our race, ethnicity and culture. Along with our intergenerational education about bowing to white authority, many of us will have been raised with cultural norms such as not interrupting, being humble, respecting elders, being obedient and not pushing boundaries. While these in themselves are not necessarily bad things, many of them *are* at odds with Western norms, which can make it difficult for us to stand in our power when confronted with unfair or disrespectful treatment.

For example, an area that comes up a lot in my sessions is self-advocacy in the workplace. I've worked with lots of Black and brown professionals who feel that they are not able to challenge bosses or older colleagues, due to a genuine desire to respect their elders. Respecting elders in a family or community context is a beautiful thing, but as first-, second- or third-generation immigrants, we need to learn how to integrate our cultural upbringing with the Western environments in which we live. You can still respect the aunties, uncles and grandparents in your community while *also* knowing you have the right to challenge others regardless of their age.

> **REFLECTIVE MOMENT**
>
> Respecting your elders and respecting yourself are not mutually exclusive. Think about the cultural values you have grown up with that may be impacting your ability to assert yourself. Consider how you would like to integrate them in a Western context.

Speaking up in the workplace is of utmost importance. Work is where we spend most of our time, and for many of us, it's a place where we derive a lot of meaning and purpose. If you're faced with prejudice at work, having an awareness of your organizational policies and procedures around discrimination and anti-racism is imperative. Knowing your rights will help you navigate the system and record your complaints properly. It's also invaluable to keep a log of discriminatory or racist incidents and experiences, including dates, times, location, overview and witnesses, and if you need support, reach out to a trusted colleague, HR partner, or diversity and inclusion officer within your company.

Allyship
Another important thing to consider in the journey of advocacy and equality is allyship. An ally is someone who supports and advocates for members of marginalized or underrepresented groups. For example, I try my best to be an ally for the disabled community. I try to stay educated and informed about disability awareness, promote inclusion and challenge discriminatory practices when I see them.

For white allies, this does not simply mean being "not racist" – it is being actively anti-racist and having a willingness to use their privilege and influence to challenge inequality. A major part of allyship is confronting internal biases and continuing education to support positive change.

Allyship is not, however, speaking on behalf of marginalized groups or "saving" them. It is standing side by side to provide advocacy and support. The term "white saviour" refers to white people who feel they have a role to play in "rescuing" or "liberating" people of colour. I remember seeing this a lot in my childhood, when white celebrities would go to countries in Africa and Asia to "help" the communities and share their experiences with the media. Their trips would include taking photos of local children without consent and making cringeworthy statements about how happy these communities were, "despite having so little".

This the exact opposite of allyship. White saviourism views non-white people as passive victims. However, allyship views people of global majority as equals and stems from a place of empathy, humanity and solidarity.

CASE STUDY: Allyship in action

Louise is a 35-year-old white woman of British heritage. She is a physiotherapist by trade, considers herself an open-minded person and has friends from many diverse cultural backgrounds.

In 2020, Louise began to research anti-racism and realized that despite her open-minded nature, she had internalized some unaddressed racial and cultural stereotypes that she wanted to unpick.

> During a shift at work, Louise became aware of a colleague talking in a derogatory manner about patients for whom English was not their first language. This made Louise feel uncomfortable, particularly as she worked in a multicultural team.
>
> In the past, Louise would have kept her head down and stayed away from this person. However, this time, Louise chose to address the issue with her colleague and privately check in on members of the team who may have taken personal offence.
>
> Unfortunately, Louise's colleague stood by their discriminatory comments, and as a result, she chose to report them to senior management. When Louise came to me, she was understandably distressed by the situation but felt proud that she was an active BIPOC ally and no longer a bystander to prejudice and hate.

I have friends from a wide range of backgrounds, both from the global minority and majority, who would consider themselves not racist. However, there are only a certain few who I believe are active *allies* for my community, and these are the type of people who are key when it comes to gaining support and fighting the good fight.

It's important to know who the allies are in our communities, but we can also work toward active allyship within ourselves. We too have discrimination toward one another in our global-majority communities (more on this later!), so it is also up to us to advocate for those who may come from different backgrounds to our own, and for those who may also be facing microaggressions.

DEVELOPING SYSTEMS TO SELF-SOOTHE

Although you have the right to challenge, speak out and disagree with others, it's imperative to recognize that there are times when you'll feel unable to speak up. Maybe the environment is too hostile, perhaps you are greatly outnumbered, or maybe you just don't want to put yourself in the firing line.

I'm not here to victim-shame, and I too have had experiences where I've felt unable to fully express myself (such as the swimming pool saga I shared at the start of this book, when I could do little more than cry). Your self-care is paramount, and a big part of looking after yourself is to make the judgement call as to whether speaking out is in your best interest.

One way to feel more comfortable with holding firm boundaries is to set yourself mini boundaries tests. Think of a relatively low-stakes area of your life, within which you could practise holding boundaries. Let's say you decide to do this socially. This could mean that you're honest about which restaurant you really want to go to, you tell a friend you're upset if they're late, or you turn down an invitation for an event that you don't want to attend. By practising holding boundaries outside of microaggressions, you can draw on your improved skills in more challenging situations.

> **REFLECTIVE MOMENT**
>
> Think about some of the difficult feelings or emotions that may prevent you from asserting yourself in uncomfortable situations. What can you do to mitigate them?

Even if you are a confident person who is adept at holding boundaries, being on the receiving end of microaggressions can challenge the best of us. I would consider myself a confident person, but in the face of microaggressions, there are still times when I find it difficult to assert myself. Luckily, holding boundaries is a skill like any other – with practice, it gets easier.

Having said that, dealing with microaggressions can be emotionally draining, especially over a prolonged period. Consider what support you need to help you through – for example, spending time with friends or family, seeking therapeutic support or making lifestyle improvements, such as scheduling time to exercise, picking up new hobbies or preparing nourishing food.

> ### **TOP TIP:** Develop a self-care plan
>
> Sometimes, when we experience stressful events, it can be hard to know what to do to make ourselves feel better. Developing a self-care plan can be a tool to draw on during tough times.
>
> Make a list of the following as a starter:
>
> 1. What **physical self-care activities** support me the most?
>   E.g., exercising, having a massage, cooking for myself, having a bath
> 2. What **emotional self-care practices** help me look after my emotional wellbeing?
>   E.g., journaling, going to therapy, talking to friends, being creative

3. What **social self-care activities** help me to feel good?
   E.g., volunteering, seeing friends, spending time with family
4. What types of **leisurely self-care pursuits** bring me the most joy?
   E.g., watching films or TV, walking, crafting, playing sports
5. What **spiritual observations** help foster a sense of inner peace?
   E.g., spending time in nature, or practising gratitude, prayer or meditation

You can tweak and amend your self-care plan as you see fit and depending on what you need in the moment.

Along with performing self-care regularly, it is important to implement aftercare in the aftermath of distressing events. Aftercare refers to activities specifically undertaken following a challenging experience, and it's an essential part of healing and recovery. Tapping into your self-care plan can form a big part of your aftercare, but you also have a variety of embodied tools – practices that use the body to cultivate self-healing – that you can use to relieve stress during mentally and emotionally demanding times.

TOP TIP: Relieve stress in the moment with embodied methods

The following techniques can support the body in stressful moments, helping to relieve tension and calm the nervous system.

1. **Shaking:** Find a comfortable and private space. Stand with your feet hip-width apart, bring your attention to your body and take a few deep breaths. Allow any tension in your body to release and slowly begin shaking. Start with one or two body parts, and then let it spread across your whole body. Let the movement be spontaneous and free. When you feel ready, start to slow down, and bring your body to a standstill. Take a few deep breaths and notice any shifts or physical sensations you feel.
2. **Crying:** Crying can help to let go and shift intense or blocked emotions. If your tears don't come naturally, you can elicit them by journaling about your emotions, listening to sad music or watching sad media. Give yourself full permission to release!
3. **Using your voice:** When you feel voiceless, unheard or unseen, your voice can be one of the first things to suffer. You can explore speaking to an empty chair and getting it all out, singing at the top of your lungs, or having a good scream into a pillow or soundproofed space. Ensure you are somewhere safe, comfortable and private for this one – you may want to journal afterwards to explore how it felt to use your voice in this way.

Another important part of aftercare is reflection. During a hurtful incident, it can be difficult to process everything that you are experiencing. Afterwards, emotional processing can help you to reflect on what happened, acknowledge how you feel and decide what actions you need to take next. It can help you assess any unhelpful beliefs that may have cropped up (e.g., "I'm overreacting"), and things that you did well (e.g., speaking up despite being nervous). Reflecting can help gain a broader perspective and provide a springboard for conversations with others if additional support is needed. Reflection can also help with the process of closure. It allows you the space to process any unresolved emotions and make peace with what has happened. This is particularly important if an apology or actual closure with the person is not likely.

> ## REFLECTIVE MOMENT
>
> Journaling after a challenging event can be a useful tool for self-reflection.
> Here are some prompts to try if you want to use writing to help you process a difficult experience:
> - What happened?
> - How did I feel physically, mentally and emotionally?
> - How have I felt since?
> - Have my feelings about the following changed since the event? If so, how?
>   - The world
>   - The person/people involved
>   - My organization or the location where the event took place
> - How has my sense of self changed since the event?
> - What did I do in this situation that made me feel proud of myself?
> - What would I do differently if this situation arose again?
> - What can I do to best support myself now?

A final piece of the puzzle I'd like to share with you is self-compassion, the ability to treat oneself with kindness, care, understanding and acceptance. Often, when faced with hardship, the first person we turn on is ourselves. There is no right way to deal with prejudice, and there will be times when the best way to look after yourself is simply to extend the same care to yourself that you would gift to others.

Every day, you are trying the best you can, and on those days, when things don't go the way you would like, you can use any of the tools described in this chapter to help you learn and move forward.

> **TAKE CARE TAKEAWAYS**
> - Microaggressions are everyday slights and slurs directed toward people who may be marginalized.
>   o They can be difficult to recognize but your gut will guide you.
> - Advocating for yourself can come in the form of holding firm boundaries, speaking up, choosing your battles and protecting your peace.
> - Allyship is a powerful tool for change – finding your allies and building your allyship skills is vital.
> - Self-soothing can be achieved through self-care, self-reflection and self-compassion, and by using embodied tools and seeking support.

2

OVERCOMING OTHERING

WHAT DOES IT MEAN TO BE THE OTHER?

I'm a born and bred Londoner, so I have grown up in a very multicultural environment. In my primary school class, I was one of three or so Black children, and there were many others from varying different cultures, ethnicities and religious backgrounds.

As I got older, my experience of being in predominantly white spaces increased, particularly due to my interest in wellbeing and the arts. During my studies, I went from being in a very mixed GCSE Drama group to a homogenous white middle-class A-Level class. I went from mixed community gym and dance classes to all-white yoga spaces, and I went from a diverse, cosmopolitan psychology degree to an all-white postgraduate coaching course.

The older I got, the more I found myself as the other, the singular, the interloper. Most of the times, I dealt with it okay, and people were warm and friendly enough, but there was still a level of discomfort that I felt due to being perceived as different.

I recall attending a contemporary dance class not too long before writing this book and feeling somewhat exposed because I was the only melanated person in the room. The group was smiley and friendly, as was the teacher, but nearly everyone was of the same age range, body type and even hair colour! I stuck out like a sore thumb. The teacher instructed us to turn to the person next to us and introduce ourselves. Despite being stood smack-bang in the middle of the studio, every single participant turned to someone else other than me. I felt like a kid stuck on the side on a school sports day. I felt so embarrassed that no one seemed to want to partner with me, and in the end, I had to pair with the teacher.

Now, I am sure none of these women did anything intentionally, but I can infer that my visible difference made it so that I wasn't the obvious choice for connection in the room. It left me feeling deflated, self-conscious and awkward. I never went back to that class again, and as a result, I'm sure I've missed out on what could have been a great dance experience.

To be the other is to be an outsider within the existence of an "in-group" and an "out-group". Essentially, it's an "us-vs-them" attitude. This sense of "us vs them" can be either conscious or subconscious, and often the development of unequal systems are based on creating this type of mentality.

Even though no one likes being on the outside, there is an innate human desire for things to be grouped into categories – it's quite primal. There is also a strong internal drive to feel a connection with those who are like us. How many times have you felt an unexplained attachment to a celebrity who you have never met, but who has a similar background? Or been abroad and met someone from your hometown and felt an instant bond? (For me, this is an instinctual connection to mega-star Rihanna simply because she hails from the same island as me.)

This is all quite normal. However, issues arise when someone who identifies strongly with a particular group begins to attribute specific traits to the other, and therefore starts seeing one as better and the other as worse. This can result in a multi-layered and deep bias toward those perceived to be on the other side.

We see this play out a lot in our daily lives: at work (employees vs management); at school (popular kids vs the outcasts); in neighbourhoods (private owners vs social housing); and, of course, within the realm of race, culture and ethnicity.

Governments and institutions in power have used this approach for many years to create and sustain conflict among various groups. United people are a threat to power; therefore, it makes sense that power-hungry institutions would want to keep the masses as subservient and downtrodden as possible, as twisted as that sounds. These narratives are largely driven by the media, which tells us who is "in" and who is "out". An example of this can be seen when figureheads blame immigrant populations for "taking our jobs" instead of focusing on administrations that could provide unemployment support. This is a top-down approach, and the system of oppression thrives off telling us who is better and who is worse, rather than actually fixing the problem.

This relates to race, culture and ethnicity, as for thousands of years, the Western colonial system was based on the notion that white people were superior and that people of colour were inferior. Although we may feel we have moved on from this narrative, these types of entrenched prejudices take years to disassemble, and we are still seeing the result of these archaic views to this day.

On a societal level, othering can lead to the ostracism and systemic dehumanization of whole groups of people. I remember this happening in the 2010s following 9/11, the 7/7 bombings, and the terrorist attacks in Paris and Brussels. Following these events, the US implemented the INS Special Registration, a system that required males from a range of predominantly Arab and Muslim countries to report to the government for fingerprinting. Similarly, in 2017, President Trump put a highly discriminatory travel ban into place, restricting people from Iran, Iraq, Libya, Somalia, Sudan, Syria and Yemen from entering the US (BBC).

At the time, Western governments and the media conflated terrorism with Islam and created an us-vs-them narrative portraying the West as the brave and noble saviour, and the Middle East and Islam as a space for dictatorship and evil. Of course, this was inaccurate, but it did not stop high levels of discrimination and prejudice toward Muslims and those perceived as Muslims.

I started my wellbeing business in 2009, and at that time, most of my work was based in community settings. I remember an occasion when I hired a hall for women's only dance classes. I requested that no male staff members enter the space during the session because female participants who wore hijab would be present. I was shocked to be told that "they" should learn to integrate more, and I was asked, "Aren't they forbidden from dancing anyway?"

Needless to say, I felt completely disgusted. I apologized profusely to my class attendees and proceeded to book a different hall for the remainder of the course.

This experience is a specific example of how societal othering can filter down and impact us on an individual level. When someone is othered, they can be treated with contempt, and consciously or unconsciously be perceived to be lesser than the majority group. On a more basic level, it could be as simple as being socially excluded from a space. For example, if a manager organizes a wine-tasting night for the Christmas party, those who do not drink for cultural, religious or health reasons may feel othered.

Societal and individual othering are intricately linked and are both equally as dangerous. Being othered because of race can have a major impact on an individual's lifestyle and outcomes. A study tested this premise by sending out 13,000 fake applications to job recruiters. Researchers found that there were significantly lower call-back rates for people with "ethnic-sounding" names compared to white-sounding names, despite the fake applicants all having similar credentials (Oreopoulos).

REFLECTIVE MOMENT

Where in our society have you seen an "us-vs-them" mentality play out? Consider educational spaces, the workplace, community and cultural groups, etc. What are some of the pros and cons you've noticed with having an "in" and an "out" group?

A further study into the connection between employment and race highlighted that those in everyday jobs, such as employment agents, car salespeople and real estate agents, could gatekeep careers, cars and housing for those in the position of other. For example, the study found that employment agents encouraged African American folks toward lower-paid jobs, and real estate agents showed properties in racially segregated areas to clients of colour. This study also showed that white people were more likely to be in the gatekeeping role, which highlights the great impact that being the other can have – it's an important element of a person of colour's lived experience, one that is hard to ignore (Corra).

I remember I once had dinner with a friend who had recently moved from Kenya to the UK. She had started a new job and was navigating her way through British life. We spoke about cultural integration, and I was interested to hear her thoughts on the UK so far.

"Lildonia," she said to me, "I didn't know I was Black until I moved to the UK. Back home in Kenya, I was free to just be me."

That sentence alone is one of the most powerful I've ever heard, and one of the clearest examples of how not being the other can create an incomparable level of psychological freedom.

I have my own experience of living in different countries. However, most of my experience has been based in white Western spaces. My father worked in Utrecht, Holland, for a brief period when I was younger, and I recall starting nursery in the Netherlands in the 1990s. I was three years old, and I distinctly remember feeling like an alien surrounded by all these children and adults who spoke words I'd never heard before.

My Dad had dropped me off, and the teachers had welcomed me warmly, but it was clear I was somehow different. They spoke in hushed whispers and looked at me with a mix of intrigue and trepidation. On my very first day, when I tried to join in a game of trains, the two lads I approached had other ideas. As soon as I drew near, one of them smashed a toy train firmly into my face, bursting my top lip. The nursery staff were distraught and apologized profusely to my father, but I don't remember going back to that nursery again.

That was the first experience I can remember of being othered, at the tender age of three years old. Some would say it was also my first experience of racism. We may think that these things do not affect children, but even pre-verbal incidents can have a major impact.

There has been a wide range of research carried out, which has found that children perceive and experience racial difference from a very young age. A report by the social justice organization Teaching for Change noted that babies as young as six months old are interested in differences in skin colour and gender (Teaching for Change).

I know I have witnessed white babies staring at me with intrigue and confusion when I've been travelling. This in and of itself is not a bad thing, but from about two years old, they become curious about difference, and by two and a half, they have begun to absorb societal messaging about what that difference means. As a result, teasing or isolation of children who have different skin colour, who are non-native language speakers or who have a disability can start at a very young age.

One of the most famous studies on discrimination in childhood is Jane Elliott's "Blue eyes/Brown eyes" study, which she carried out in 1968. Elliott was a primary school teacher, and the day after Dr Martin Luther King Jr was assassinated, she decided to experiment on the children in her third-grade class. She split them up into two groups: the blue eyes and the brown eyes. Blue-eyed children were told that they were smarter and superior to those with brown eyes and were given special privileges, such as longer playtime.

Those in the "superior" group became bossy and arrogant, while those in the "inferior" group became timid and subservient, and ended up achieving poorer grades. In a documentary called *The Eye of the Storm*, Elliott described how the dynamic changed among her students. She said, "I have watched wonderful, thoughtful children turn into nasty, vicious, discriminating little third graders" (Elliott).

Elliott completed various versions of this experiment throughout her years as a teacher, both with children and adults, and the results are similar across the board. This iconic study highlights how easy it is to turn people against each other based on arbitrary traits, and the near-immediate impact that being in the in-group can have.

CASE STUDY: Bias in early education

Julie is a 65-year-old white British social work manager. She considers herself to be open-minded, progressive, liberal and anti-racist.

◢ Julie had raised her children to be allies to people of colour, and was a member of her organization's Equality, Diversity and Inclusion Network. She was a supportive grandmother and babysat her granddaughter a few evenings per week.

When Julie came to see me, she was concerned at language she was hearing from her six-year-old granddaughter, who had begun making disparaging comments about Black people. Julie was shocked, horrified and worried, and didn't know how to address it.

I supported Julie by workshopping conversations she could have with her daughter and granddaughter to unpick these comments and start introducing age-appropriate anti-racism education.

Through their conversations, Julie uncovered that during Black History Month, her granddaughter had learned about apartheid from a teacher seemingly unversed in anti-racism. From the lesson, the young girl had surmised that Black people are bad and deserve to be punished.

This example illustrates not only the importance of calling in expertise to educate, but also how easy it is for children to absorb messaging about race – both negative and positive.

These examples are not only relevant to children and young people. I remember speaking with a white British friend and chatting about a mutual friend we thought we both knew. I described her as having brown hair, and being average height and Italian. My friend proceeded to say, "Oh no, surely, she's not Italian? I thought she was just normal!" In that instant, I knew that my friend had internalized thought patterns about "us" (English) vs "them" (Europeans).

Experiences such as these assure me that my nursery experience was neither a fluke nor unrelated to race and cultural differences. Further, for me, the feeling of being the other did not stop in preschool. Unfortunately, it was just the beginning. When my family returned to the UK, and I joined a mainstream British primary school, I was constantly othered, often, in very subtle ways. For example, the school nurse once tried to drag a nit comb created for Caucasian hair through my fluffy afro. I would also skip swimming lessons so I wouldn't have to deal with everyone asking me why I was carrying around a family-sized tub of cocoa butter. And people at school would make microaggressive comments, asking me if I cooked "Jamaican" food at home, or if "Dad was around". I was only young, but I noticed these differences, and from spending time delivering wellbeing services in schools and youth provisions, I know that sadly, there are many children and young people still experiencing this. In Chapter 1, we discussed the impact of microaggressions, and although they're not the same as othering, spaces where individuals are othered can become a breeding ground for microaggressions.

One would hope that as we age, the feeling of being othered diminishes, but it can become *more* acute as we enter higher education and the workplace. In my case, I did not encounter another mental health and wellbeing professional who was from a similar background for years. In training courses, I was the only melanated person, and all the media related to health and wellbeing seemed to show blonde, skinny, white women, which strengthened the belief that to be a health professional, you needed to be both skinny and white.

CASE STUDY: Being othered in education

Jacques is a 23-year-old Black British male student of Senegalese descent. He came to see me during the first few weeks of university. After moving onto campus, he found himself in an all-white block of student halls and instantly felt like the odd one out.

He described how his flatmates would often speak to him in "Black British slang", some of which he didn't understand, and as a result, he felt the need to exaggerate his Blackness to fit the image of him they'd created in their minds. He'd rarely get invited to night outs, and although he could not prove it, his deep internal sense was that they perceived him as different because of his ethnicity.

CASE STUDY: Being othered at work

Nishaan is a 35-year-old Sri Lankan British-born male. He was born in and raised in Kent, and in his thirties, he took up a research post in the North of England.

As soon as he started working with his new team, he felt out of sorts. No one tried to talk to him or get to know him. He didn't understand their banter, and his colleagues rarely invited him on nights out, assuming he wouldn't want to attend pubs or clubs due to his ethnicity and perceived religious beliefs.

> Nishaan would actively try to engage, inviting colleagues out for coffee or finding ways to bond over work tasks, but it simply didn't work. He felt left out, homesick and on the outside of a team that he had been very excited to join. In the end, he found his place in the UK through activities outside of work, meet-up groups and connecting with the Sri Lankan community in his new area.
>
> In my final session with Nishaan, he felt relieved that he'd managed to find a community, but still felt socially excluded at work, the environment where he spent most of his time.

Sometimes when we feel othered, it can be difficult to name the experience. In the examples mentioned, neither Nishaan nor Jacques was directly told that they didn't fit in. It was more a sense and a subtle feeling. This can make it hard to name, identify or even accept what is happening. People of colour have been told for many years that they've got a "chip on their shoulder", or a perceived negative attitude because they've been mistreated. Not acknowledging this mistreatment – and instead blaming the recipient for feeling badly for having experienced it – can lead people to question themselves or fear not being believed.

I recall having a conversation with a white colleague during my peer supervision group who asked what I would advise when working with clients who present with racial trauma. My first and foremost piece of advice was to *believe them*. For many racialized people, having to justify discriminatory experiences is commonplace, and that in and of itself can be extremely distressing.

Unfortunately, stories like Nishaan's and Jacques's are not uncommon, and in my coaching practice, I hear countless stories from people of colour about how they feel like they don't belong in white spaces. One of the most powerful things I can do is to simply listen and *believe*.

Being part of a subgroup can be challenging, and often in modern media, minority communities face criticism and backlash for not "integrating" into mainstream Western society. However, as we can see, it is not as easy as simply slipping into place. It is of comfort to be in spaces where you feel you belong, and for many, it is easier to prosper within one's own community than in the mainstream.

We see this in the reverse throughout the world when white Western expats create entire expatriate communities abroad without ever integrating into their host countries. We accept this as a normal part of life, but when Black and brown people do the same thing, they are often villainized.

We have moved beyond the legal framework of segregation, but the impact of othering leads to an invisible line that can lead people of colour to feel on the outside of society. Only once the mainstream culture recognizes these difficulties and makes genuine efforts to be more welcoming and embrace differences can we work toward a truly inclusive society.

TOP TIP: Repeat affirmations for empowerment

When feeling othered, using positive affirmations can be both sustaining and validating.

Encouraging statements about your place in the world can help you overcome doubt, negative thoughts and fear of disapproval.

> You can say them out loud or in your head, or you can write them down. You can create your own, or give these examples a try:
>
> 1. I have a right to be here.
> 2. I belong.
> 3. I add value to the world.
> 4. I am allowed to take up space.
> 5. My uniqueness is a gift.

Being on the outside can be very fatiguing. Humans are tribal creatures, and we thrive in community with others. For our distant ancestors, being different could have cost them their lives, so it makes sense that our evolutionary driver wants us to fit in. Of course, there are always going to be differences between us as individuals, but the system of white supremacy means that, for culturally diverse people, the cost of not fitting in is immense.

Everyone deals with being othered differently. There is no right or wrong way to be excluded. For some, being bold in the face of othering works, but for others, compliance is the most secure self-protection vehicle. When we suffer persistent experiences of being othered, we can lose our voices and become silenced, which can reinforce stereotypes around BIPOC's abilities. This may mean you keep your head down to avoid "causing a fuss" or bow to authority without question.

Another potential impact of being the other is developing "double consciousness". This term was coined by historian and sociologist W. E. B. Du Bois in the late 18th century. Du Bois spoke of the psychological and identity challenges that African Americans experienced due to racism, marginalization and othering they experienced in the US. Having a double consciousness means to have two simultaneous experiences of the world: one that correlates with how an individual sees themselves based on their own culture and personal experiences, and the other which personifies how society views them, often with stereotypes and prejudice (Du Bois).

I can resonate with this – growing up, I was all too aware of the negative stereotypes surrounding young Black people, particularly those from working-class backgrounds. Perceptions of criminality, anti-social behaviour and lack of education were just a few of the stereotypes I faced. However, deep inside, I knew I was none of these things. This was further corroborated when I went to Africa for the first time and revelled at being perceived as just "a person" without all the baggage that comes with being Black in the UK.

In his writing, Du Bois mentioned some of the potential negative impacts of a double consciousness, including internalizing negative views of oneself, an internal conflict between both identities, emotional strain and alienation from broader society.

Although this theory was developed specifically in relation to African Americans in the 19th and 20th centuries, I'm sure many people from global-majority backgrounds can resonate with this feeling. Something that people of colour commonly do to fit in with white norms is "code-switch". This term was initially coined to refer to linguistics and the ability to switch between two languages or language varieties, and can be both conscious and unconscious. POCs, however, code-switch to adjust the way they look, behave and express themselves in order to "fit in" with the dominant culture, or to make others feel comfortable.

For me, while growing up, I learned to code-switch between standard English and Black British vocabulary. In the UK, using Black British, African British or Caribbean British dialect is perceived as "slang". Many non-Black young people now use words from the African diasporic lexicon, and as a result, it has become synonymous with "street language".

Of course, there is nothing "street" about these vernaculars – they're simply dialects like any other. However, due to negative stereotyping, I have, over the years, felt I've had to dull down my "Blackness" and Black Caribbean speech to fit in majority-white spaces. We can see this within other minority groups, too, when people feel that they must switch up their "cultural" selves, depending on their environment.

Alongside code-switching there are many ways in which people change their behaviours, emotional responses, personalities and overall demeanours to fit in with the wider group. This is known as masking, and often, people may not even realize they're doing it. Constantly having to suppress or mask elements of yourself can cause exhaustion, internal disharmony, and both physical and psychological health problems.

CASE STUDY: Hidden identity

Jenny is British born with roots in Hong Kong. At the time I worked with her, she was a 24-year-old graduate entering the workplace for the first time.

▲ Jenny was very proud of her heritage and enjoyed participating in cultural rituals, routines and traditions. However, starting her first job, Jenny found herself embarrassed of displaying her Chinese culture in front of colleagues. She'd often downplay her weekend activities and changed her eating habits to bring in more anglicized food in her packed lunch. Anytime she had to mention anything connected to her East Asian heritage, she would cringe and try her best to change the subject.

Things changed for Jenny when an older colleague joined the team from the Japanese division. Jenny was both shocked and inspired to see her colleague speak proudly about being East Asian and eat her lunch out of a traditional Japanese bento box with chopsticks. For Jenny, it was a monumental moment.

This colleague had a long and successful career in both Asia and Europe, and it taught Jenny that she didn't need to dull down her Asian-ness to progress in the workplace.

Code-switching, masking and attempting to blend in are essentially survival tools, and it can be exhausting to constantly feel that you should amend elements of your core being just to survive. It is the Black woman feeling she has to straighten her hair, the Muslim person feeling like they cannot ask for a designated prayer space, the Asian woman feeling she needs to "prove" she's not submissive, or the Black man making an effort to show that he's not aggressive.

The reason code-switching exists is because of the stereotypes around marginalized cultures that are deeply embedded within our society. If these didn't exist, cultural differences would be valued and celebrated, or at a bare minimum, accepted as a part of life in the same way as people accept differences in eye and hair colour.

This feeling of being othered due to one's race or ethnicity is something that people of colour specifically face. As we saw with the Blue eyes/Brown eyes study mentioned earlier in the chapter, those in the out-group had almost instant changes in their demeanour and attainment. Othering is not only deeply uncomfortable, but it also has an impact on self-esteem, self-realization and achievement levels.

When in a discussion about racism with an old colleague, I remember her likening being white while travelling in Africa to being Black in a majority-white country. She described being stared at and not fitting in, and she despised feeling like the odd one out. However, white supremacy was created for the advancement of white people; therefore, being "the solo white person" can often afford you privileges and status that being the sole person of colour cannot.

We just need to look at countries across the melanated diaspora that have white minority communities, such as South Africa, Kenya, Zimbabwe and Brazil. Despite making up a small section of the population, these communities hold a disproportionate amount of wealth, status and privilege compared to the Black and brown natives.

Being othered can further impact the psyche by causing someone to develop a dislike or mistrust of white people. This can happen because of one's direct experiences of being othered or racial trauma, or through stories passed down from generation to generation (we'll discuss this more later). This can manifest as people not engaging with mainstream society, experiencing extreme anger or fear, or taking part in reverse discrimination.

CASE STUDY: Mistrust of white people

Samuel is of mixed Afro-Grenadian and White British Heritage. Growing up, he did not know his father and was raised in a rural part of the UK. During his childhood, he gave little thought to his racial identity. However, when attending secondary school, he became increasingly aware of his difference.

Samuel would often receive comments about his appearance, and at one point was sent home from school for wearing his afro loose. His hometown had a strong contingent of the British National Party (a far-right fascist political party), and he grew increasingly uncomfortable walking the streets for fear of race-related violence.

Samuel began to research far-right ideology and colonial history and developed a strong distrust of both England and white people. He began to get into arguments with friends and family members who were right-leaning and found it difficult to share his cultural evolution with his white mother.

I worked with Samuel to find coping strategies for the racial trauma he had endured. I also supported him to find non-violent ways to channel his anger (e.g., through activism and peaceful protest).

> I also supported him in honing the tools needed to maintain relationships with people in his life while also speaking his truth about the difficulties of growing up as a mixed-heritage young person in a racist area.

Being othered can also lead to a level of shame. The difference between shame and embarrassment is that embarrassment is related to something you have done, while shame is to feel disgrace about who you are as a person.

Experiencing social exclusion can breed feelings of low self-esteem and create a deep-seated belief that you're unworthy. This lack of belonging can impact confidence and affect how you perceive yourself, your relationships, your personality, your appearance and indeed your cultural identity. All these things combined can result in mental health difficulties such as anxiety, depression and self-harm, with many people struggling to find an outlet for their emotions.

Stop Hate UK's 2020/2021 report stated that nearly half of their calls were related to racial hatred, and of those, 38 per cent were from individuals disclosing their ethnicity as Asian – a jump from the previous year, when 16 per cent of calls came from this community. The report also stated that hate crimes had risen by a shocking 73 per cent overall in 2021 with a total of 82,268 racially aggravated offences recorded between 2020–2021 (Stop Hate UK). This report goes to show that people of colour are constantly confronted with the harsh reality that they are still not fully accepted in the countries where they live.

CASE STUDY: Mental health and being othered

Jude is a Vietnamese-born, British-raised transracial adoptee who was brought to the UK at three years old to live with her white adoptive family.

Jude had a loving upbringing and close relationship with her parents and siblings. However, she was acutely aware of her difference as the only Asian member of the family. Jude was one of the few people of colour in her community too, and as she grew older, she began to feel more and more like an outsider.

Jude states that she never had any direct experiences of discrimination or racism growing up, but rather that there was just an underlying feeling that she was different. Jude did not enjoy family events or pictures, as they simply reflected her loneliness.

As Jude entered adolescence, she began to have increased levels of anxiety. She became worried that she would never fit in and began to have feelings of low self-worth. Eventually, at the age of 18, she received a diagnosis of anxiety and depression. She would often self-harm to relieve the mental pressure.

During her time at university, she began to see a therapist, and I became her wellbeing coach. These appointments, combined with access to multicultural groups, allowed Jude to be able to work toward acceptance of her culture of origin and ethnicity. However, whenever Jude visited her hometown during the holidays, the feelings began to re-emerge, and her symptoms worsened.

Jude continues to work on coping strategies to manage her mental health and release her trauma around feeling different.

WAYS TO EMBRACE YOUR UNIQUENESS

One of the most important factors in overcoming othering is to find ways to embrace who you truly are. The feeling of fully accepting yourself is empowering, liberating and extremely inspirational to those around you. Although it can be difficult, I would urge you to try and express at least some elements of your whole self without downplaying your difference. I can assure you that the possibility of an empowered and multifaceted identity is possible.

There were so many years when I was hidden in my Blackness, subconsciously viewing my authentic Black self as something only to be shared around those I was very close to or other Black people. Now, I am loud and proud about who I am. I still love learning about and engaging with other cultures, but I am unapologetic in celebrating who I am. I love my Black culture, I love my mixed ancestry, I love my African heritage, and anyone who does not accept and embrace that about me should not be in my life.

TOP TIP: Make a list

If you experience comparison, self-doubt or low self-esteem when being the other, make a list of things that you're good at, ways in which you've excelled and your top achievements.

Keep this list on your phone, add to it often and pull it out every time that self-doubt starts to creep in.

It's time for us, as a global-majority community, to make a change. The more of us that allow our cultural identities to shine, the more space there will be for the next generation to do the same. I love seeing schools' international celebration days, when children come in dressed in traditional attire and carrying plates heaped with their cultural cuisine. It may seem inconsequential, but it's so important for children to receive the message that who they are culturally and who they're expected to be in a public space can happily co-exist.

> **REFLECTIVE MOMENT**
>
> Think about ways in which you can actively be proud of your culture in the public domain, whether that's making sure your name is pronounced correctly, making time for prayer or taking days off for faith-based holidays. If these things are important to you, they must remain part of your life. Make a list of as many things that you can think of, and then start to perform them wherever you go.

Alongside highlighting your individuality, I encourage you to try not to downplay your otherness. Minimizing your uniqueness does not work – it simply creates resentment and low self-esteem. I acknowledge that it takes a lot of work to deconstruct the negative messages you may have been fed about your race, culture, faith and difference, but it's a journey that we all must go on because we belong, and we are beautiful! Your uniqueness is your superpower, and although it may not seem like it at times, there are so many ways that your heritage and cultural experience can be of benefit.

Growing up, there were elements of being of mixed heritage that I felt were somewhat challenging. I never came across others with African American or Native American heritage, and I hadn't grown up in a traditional Caribbean home like most of my Caribbean peers. Most people I came across who were half Caribbean were mixed white British, and often I felt like I didn't have my own "space".

However, I have now realized that my mixed cultural background is a huge asset. Being exposed to multiple cultures growing up has made me culturally inquisitive and accepting of others. And in my work now, being able to engage with others across the spectrum of race, culture and background is an asset. In fact, many of the clients I work with comment on how understood they feel being supported by a multicultural woman of colour. In other words, something I'd perceived as a flaw is now my unique selling point.

REFLECTIVE MOMENT

List all the things from your background that you find difficult to express in a majority-white setting.

Take a moment to go through each one and think about how you can use that trait as a superpower. How do your unique and distinctive qualities help you out in different scenarios and within different relationships?

CASE STUDY: Bringing your true self to work

Adam is Jordan born and London raised. His faith is a monumental part of his life, but he felt that he could not show it at work. So, for years, Adam hid his faith as much as possible, choosing not to pray or fast at work and, where possible, not disclosing that he was a Muslim. There were times during his career when he felt it safer to lay low, particularly during times when Islamophobia was rife in the UK.

Even in "safer" and more diverse teams, he still found it difficult to integrate this part of himself at work.

This began to grate on Adam. He felt incongruent, and he felt that his spiritual connection was weakening. When he came to see me, his anxiety was at an all-time high. He felt like a fraud both at work and at home.

I worked with Adam to explore how he could bring together these two parts of his identity in a way that felt secure. We set some small goals around joining his employer's Equality and Diversity Network, letting colleagues know why he'd be off work during Eid, and following prominent Muslim businesspeople on Instagram. Adam began to turn a corner and, over time, he realized that when he focused less on hiding who he was, he was able to perform better. His anxiety lessened, he formed stronger relationships with his colleagues, and through the company's Equality and Diversity Network, he became a mentor for new BIPOC career-starters across the company.

Adam's story is a perfect example of how being forced to hide your true self can impact both your emotional and physical wellbeing. Your uniqueness doesn't just have to refer to your cultural background – it can include being a carer, multilingual or a parent, having a chronic illness/disability, your sexual orientation, etc. These things are part of your distinctive makeup, and instead of perceiving them as a hindrance, it's important to think about how these roles can give you a distinct edge, both in the workplace and everyday life.

It's also important to connect with a diverse range of people and groups. This is particularly important if you find yourself living, working or studying in predominantly white spaces. Join people-of-colour networks, connect with forums online and find activities in an area that will expose you to various types of people. You must be able to access spaces where you feel welcome, valued and able to be your true self.

Having mentors and role models is so inspiring and shows us what is truly possible. With the internet at our disposal, we're able to seek out connections like never before. There are now a range of support groups for people from diverse communities, and this has been life-saving for many people from marginalized communities.

> **TOP TIP:** Follow in someone's footsteps
>
> If you work or study in a field where its uncommon to see people from your background, take time to find people from a similar background that do the things you do (or the things you want to do) for inspiration. Make a list of people you look up to and find out as much as possible about them, their journey and their successes.

> If they're a public figure, stay connected with them online, and if they're someone within your community, see if you can organize a coffee and chat. Note down what inspires you about this particular person, and what you can learn from their pathway.

Along with finding your kinfolk and highlighting your uniqueness, it's important to focus on the positives that your cultural upbringing has given you. When we're in the minority, it is easy to feel that there is something wrong with the way we were brought up. Mass media narratives often describe our cultures as "backwards" or in the past. However, the ancient wisdom found in our cultures is often what many aspects of Western culture are aiming to emulate or appropriate.

CASE STUDY: Embracing your whole self

Layla is a 29-year-old British born Muslim of Pakistani heritage. She has always lived in a busy and loving multi-generational household. In one way she loved being able to have a close relationship with her parents and grandparents, but in another, she felt deeply ashamed of not living independently like her white British peers.

When we delved deeper during our sessions together, we uncovered that Layla's ability to connect with elders was a skill that enabled her to connect with people of all ages. Layla also realized that maintaining close family connections was something she was proud of and would like to carry forward in her own future family.

Our cultures are rich, multifaceted and beautiful. Western values are not better – they're just different. As obvious as it may sound, there are good and bad parts to every single culture, and it is up to us to choose the elements we'd like to carry forward. When you understand (and accept) that your existence and culture are just as valid as any other, it becomes easier to let your individuality shine through.

> **REFLECTIVE MOMENT**
>
> Take a moment to think about the elements of your culture that you love, whether that's the food, music, healing modalities, cultural norms, spiritual practices or language. Sit with that, write it down and journal on why it means so much to you.

ADVICE AND TOOLS FOR DEFEATING OTHERING

We are in a uniquely powerful and progressive time, and I truly believe there is space for inclusivity to change for the better. If you'd like to expand your horizons and take up more space, there are a few pathways I would suggest. Firstly, I would like you to know that you deserve to be in any space that you choose! No environment is not right for you if it is a space your heart so desires.

At the time of writing, I have seen Olympians in hijab, South Asian American Netflix films, a Black US president, and a mixed-heritage woman as vice president. Representation is so important, and if these brave individuals did not take the steps toward accessing spaces where there was no one before them, we would not have these images to aspire to.

When I first trained as a yoga instructor, the feeling of being the other, along with imposter syndrome, would constantly creep in. I did not know any other Black yoga teachers, I had never seen another Black female in class, and the media highlighted yoga as an activity for slim white women. My body didn't look like any of the images I saw online.

Despite this, my passion for yoga shone through, and I stuck with it. Now, I am so glad I did, as many of my yoga students have told me that my presence as a diverse teacher was one of the things that encouraged them to sign up for class.

Don't get me wrong – it's an ongoing journey, and even to this day I sometimes need to give myself a "you belong here" pep talk before I enter predominantly white spaces. But I remind myself daily that I have just as much of a right to be in the spaces I choose as anyone else who's there.

> **REFLECTIVE MOMENT**
>
> Think of something you've been wanting to do for a while, but you haven't yet because you feel you won't fit in.
> - What can you do to make this aspiration a part of your reality?
> - Write down ten steps you can take to get closer to this goal.

I've mentioned this already, but BIPOC cultures have more similarities than differences, and I truly feel this is also true across the board for all humans, regardless of cultural background. Although we've been encouraged to believe that different racial groups, cultures and ethnicities are miles apart, when it comes down to it, there are countless commonalities in the human experience.

So, when I'm in spaces where I initially feel I'm the "odd one out", I seek to find similarities with others in my environment. In the wellbeing space, I am still somewhat of an oddity as a Black woman, and when I am in training groups, supervision or teams, I will often be the only woman of colour.

When this happens, I choose to focus on the things I have in common with the group, whether that's our shared passion for wellbeing, the fact we're all women or that we all have similar outlooks. I would encourage you to do this, too. When you're worried about being on the outside, it is important to find ways to build connections and ways to bridge the gap. (Please note: This *does not* include hostile spaces, but those in which you're the solo person of colour by chance.)

TOP TIP: Forge connections

If you want to feel more connected to your fellow humans, here are some things you can try:

1. **Connect with people who've got similar interests to you.** That might mean joining a social group, finding a community online or catching up with people in your professional network.

> 2. **Offer a smile.** If you're in an environment where you're feeling slightly on the edge, start with a smile and see where it leads to.
> 3. **Be vulnerable.** If you're feeling lonely, disconnected or left out, share your truth with someone you trust.
> 4. **Listen actively.** When having a conversation, take the time to truly be present, listen to what they have to say and allow them time to really share.
> 5. **Journal.** Highlight three positive connections or conversations you've had during the day. It can be a deep chat with a friend or as simple as pleasant banter with your barista on the way to the office.

When I moved from London to a small city in Italy during the pandemic, I went from living in a diverse and cosmopolitan city to a homogenous environment with very few Black and brown people. Although the city was beautiful, Italy has a long and well-known history of racism and fascism, and I often found myself on edge. Although initially feeling out of place and disconnected, I managed to find small ways to connect with people, whether through striking up a conversation with the barista I saw every day, or being social as a way to try and connect with people with similar interests. By seeking out the humanity in others, I was able to connect, make friends and build community.

We have probably all fallen prey to perpetuating the othering model, and at one point or another, we've surely succumbed to us-vs-them thinking. These situations can arise even within BIPOC groups, so we need to work hard to disassemble the messages we've been taught about who does and does not belong.

I know when I was younger, the Caribbean community and the African community did not see eye to eye, and there were stereotypes about both groups flying around left, right and centre (which is shocking and sad seeing as Afro-Caribbeans have African heritage). When I look back, I can see that, despite having many African friends growing up, there were times when I too fell into the us-vs-them mentality.

Although among my peers, Caribbeans were viewed as "cool" (thank you, Sean Paul, Beenie Man and Elephant Man for that), they weren't viewed as "serious", and we had a reputation for being loud, unprofessional and educated. My African age-mates, on the other hand, were respected educationally and professionally, but they would often be made fun of for their names, skin complexion, languages and food.

> **REFLECTIVE MOMENT**
>
> Consider ways in which you might have made another person feel othered. How can you work to be more inclusive of those who may be different to you in some way?

Funnily enough, I think the reduction in stigma came for me through music and my introduction into the world of Azonto and Afrobeats. It was the first time I saw African people in the mass media, and it encouraged me to learn more about the various cultures. Something as simple as that helped me to breakdown unconscious prejudice and my internalized unconscious bias toward African culture.

We have a responsibility, privilege and power to reduce othering within our own communities by seeking connection over competition. Finding ways to revel in your own uniqueness while celebrating others can create a powerful base for cultivating inclusive relationships.

TAKE CARE TAKEAWAYS

- To be othered is to be excluded as part of an "in-group" and "out-group".
- The impact is plentiful, with a potential negative impact on people as individuals or as part of wider groups.
- Being the other can impact our outcomes concerning employment, housing, education, finance and health.
- Being othered can force us to hide elements of ourselves, which can cause mental, emotional and psychological distress.
- You can deal with being othered by embracing your uniqueness, positive traits and accomplishments.
- Seeking out diverse role models and spaces provides a base for inspiration and support.
- Building connections with others who are different to you offers an opportunity for growth and connection.

3

COMBATTING CULTURAL CONFLICT

THE IMPACT OF A SPLIT IDENTITY

Growing up with a range of cultures can be both beautiful and confusing. Although my parents may look similar (brown skin, curly hair, brown eyes), their cultures couldn't have been more different.

My dad grew up in the suburban-like city of Anchorage, Alaska. He was born and raised in the US with mixed African, Indigenous and European heritage. His parents were pastors, and his upbringing was distinctly African American, with a focus on church, fast food and the American values of hard work, capitalism, individualism and freedom of speech. He came to the UK in the 80s on a gap year, never having experienced another country other than his own.

My mother, on the other hand, was born in the sweet and sleepy island of Barbados, but came to the UK in the 1960s as part of the Windrush generation – Caribbean immigrants who were recruited to rebuild post-war Britain. Her background is Afro-Caribbean with some Scottish heritage (due to enslavement), and she was brought up with quite opposing values to the ones my father was raised with, such as strong family ties, community cohesion, collectivism and respect for elders.

I was brought up with a combination of both cultures, along with strong ties to a Northwest London British identity. At times, I didn't know what my true identity was, or which parts of my culture felt most prevalent for me.

I know I am not alone in these complex feelings as it is something that comes up a lot when I work with BIPOC clients who live in the global north. This feeling of split identity. A clash between their culture of origin and the culture in which they reside.

Broadly speaking, Western cultures tend to be more individualistic, with a focus on the "I". Individual pursuits, goals and successes are highly prioritized and valued. However, many non-Western cultures tend to focus on the "we", with the needs of the collective (e.g., tribe, kin, country, family) considered to be more important than individual pursuits.

I noticed this difference very starkly at ten years old during my first trip "back home" to Barbados. The island is tiny, only 21 miles from top to bottom, so the sense of community is great. Everyone knows their neighbours, people greet each other when they pass in the street, they support one another, and those with less access to resources are often helped by members of the community. It was something so refreshing for me, and even at such a young age, I remember being struck by the dissimilarities in the British and Caribbean cultures.

People with multicultural upbringings will often notice major differences in emotional expression, attitudes toward mental health, rites of passage, approaches to relationships, belief systems around sex/sexuality and connection to family of origin. These differences can make it difficult for first-, second- and third-generation folks to get by in a Western context, either due to internal or external cultural value clashes.

This can sometimes lead to what is known as intergroup marginalization – the experience of rejection from your culture, for behaving in ways deemed as threatening to the social norms of the host culture. Growing up, I remember derogatory terms such as "coconut", "Bounty", "banana" or "ABCD" (American-born confused desi) being used to accuse people of being too "Westernized" or "too white".

These terms are not only highly offensive, but also completely unfounded – there is no one way to be a person of colour, and there is no such thing as a "white" Black or brown person. This can be a challenging line for us as people of colour to straddle. Often, we respect and value some aspects of our cultural upbringing while simultaneously feeling relieved to let others go.

This can be particularly relevant for those born (or raised from a very young age) outside of their country of origin. If, like me, you are second generation, your parents may have a strong connection to their home country that you simply cannot comprehend. As much as we can eat the food, practise rituals or speak a language, there is nothing like being born and raised in a country to give you a sense of identity.

I have a podcast called *Intersections*, where my co-host Harpreet Nandha and I speak to people who have overlapping identities and discuss how these facets can create barriers – and triumphs. On episode three, guest Antony Chang talked about his experiences as an East Asian mixed-heritage person raised in South Africa, New Zealand and eventually the UK. He spoke about returning to East Asia and expecting this feeling of "homecoming", being surrounded by people that looked like him. However, he found the experience to be quite different, as he was perceived as a foreigner. This is an experience many of us will relate to when visiting "back home".

Many migrant parents who journeyed to the West in the 80s and 90s were doing so as the first in their families to travel. They had no idea how the cultural integration would impact their family's identity. Some felt that their children would simply absorb their culture by osmosis (spoiler alert: that doesn't work!), and then they were horrified when their children turned their backs on homecooked food or couldn't string a sentence together in their native tongue. Others focused on assimilation – encouraging their children to reject aspects of their heritage to achieve their idea of success in the West. This wasn't always about financial gain, but sometimes about the feeling of safety that can come with blending in and keeping your head down. Countless families landed somewhere in between osmosis and assimilation, creating a contemporary blend of cultural fusion.

It's important to note that many migrant families didn't want to leave their countries of origin – it was necessary for survival. Countless families were thrust into a new land with no idea how to integrate or support their children's cultural identities. For lots of parents, it was an ongoing tussle being wanting to be who they were while simultaneously knowing they'd have to be something different to "survive" in the West.

CASE STUDY: Family expectations in relationships

Anya is a 25-year-old British-born woman with family roots in Bangladesh. Her parents moved to the UK in the 1990s, where her mother worked as a nurse and her father owned a hardware store.

Anya described her upbringing as "modern and fairly Western". Anya had friends from a variety of backgrounds, and she was pretty much allowed to come and go as she pleased. Although her family instilled a sense of Bangladeshi pride, there was little pressure to adopt cultural norms or learn her mother tongue.

When Anya was 18, she met her first boyfriend – a young Black man of the same age. Having had little pressure to maintain traditional standards, she assumed that her parents might be shocked by her choice but that, ultimately, they would support her.

Unfortunately, this was not the case. Her parents were mortified by her choice and proceeded to tell her she could not live under their roof if she continued to see her partner. They updated relatives back home who would often message Anya saying she had "sold out" or "forgotten her roots". Sadly, the pressure got to be too much, and Anya felt forced to leave a relationship that for her was a very nourishing space.

Sadly, Anya's experience is not an uncommon one, and for many there is a pressure to live a "secret" life outside of the house. This can include everything from clothing, to relationships and friendships, to sometimes even careers that parents are not aware of.

As we discussed in Chapter 2, not being able to live your truth is extremely difficult, and having to hide major aspects of our life can lead to internal conflict, anxiety and fear.

In some cases, people are not only pushed to hide from parents, but also siblings, extended family members and the wider community. When this happens, we can feel out of sync with our peers, often not feeling like a success at home, while also feeling out of loop at school, university and work. Being raised in a completely different culture to your family can make it incredibly difficult to connect and see eye to eye at times.

Many immigrant families have experienced familial separation due to factors such as parents moving abroad for work, war or civil unrest, or sending children to live with other relatives or carers for financial or educational reasons. Countless elders within our communities spent a big portion of their lives in survival mode, with financial and practical stability being at the forefront of their decision making. So, they had less access to financial, mental health and parenting support, which left many immigrant parents to just "get on with it". That, coupled with the dissolution of community due to migration and displacement, meant our parents, grandparents and other relatives had a hell of a lot to figure out.

Alternatively, Millennials and Gen Zers have been encouraged to focus on mental health and wellbeing as priority. Many of us have had access to at least some resources designed to support our personal growth and development. For our generation, an important part of this is the formation and maintenance of interpersonal relationships. That means many of us are speaking a completely different language to that of our parents. These differences can manifest as a lack of closeness, underdeveloped emotional connections or difficulty being open with parents. Many of our cultures prioritize family loyalty, which can conflict with our desire for personal freedom and autonomy. I often see this in my client cohort when adult children feel that their parents are "too strict" or "too involved" in their lives.

Sometimes, immigrant children are encouraged to repress overt displays of emotion, either to avoid "sticking out" in a white world, or because parents don't have the emotional bandwidth to take it on. Often, with the busyness of life and survival, a child's emotional needs can be neglected while the focus on security and work is overemphasized. This often leads to children being parentified, meaning they have to provide support emotionally or practically – facilitating the cultural transition, navigating bureaucracy, providing interpretation, taking on household chores, etc.

In 2019 the BBC produced a short film called *Chinese Takeaway Kids*, which focused on British Chinese children who were front-of-house in their parents' takeaway restaurants. For many immigrant children, spending time supporting the family unit before reaching working age was part and parcel of their childhoods. This support has been found to progress into adulthood for many, with about one in nine people globally being supported by funds sent home by migrant workers, and half of the money being sent to rural areas (Bó et al.).

> **CASE STUDY:** Working in the family business
>
> Mikey is a 40-year-old second-generation Korean American. During his childhood, his parents owned a Korean grocery store. Mikey remembers working in the store from as young as four years old, helping take stock, tidying and serving customers. He continued to work in the business throughout high school and also during his summer breaks once he had moved away for college. Following graduation, Mikey moved to the UK to take up a job at a well-known financial institution.
>
> While progressing with his own life and career, Mikey still felt a pressure to support his family store. Whenever he visited home for the holidays, his parents would guilt-trip him into working in the store. They'd also often ask for cash investments into the business once he started earning a salary.
>
> When Mikey came to see me, he was living in the UK and expecting his first child. He held deep compassion for his parents and respected their work ethic, but he wanted to focus on financially providing for his own family.
>
> I worked with Mikey to support him to develop his own boundaries, which included no longer working at the store during vacations and setting a yearly limit to the amount of money he would send home.

Cross-cultural upbringings may become fraught within the sphere of academic and career choices, too. Undoubtedly, our generation have had more opportunities than our parents. The world is extremely open to us in terms of education, travel, lifestyle choices, hobbies and business opportunities in a way it simply wasn't for those who raised us.

Sometimes, parents can find this evolution challenging, and this can lead to some parents trying to live out their unmet needs through their children. Whether that's encouraging them to go into a specific field of work, wanting them to end up with a specific type of partner or choosing where they live, this can be extremely difficult for people emerging into adulthood who want nothing more than to forge their own pathways. The discrepancy in views can create (or exacerbate) emotional gaps within relationships.

A 2021 study by Joblist on Gen Z, Millenials and Gen X found that, out of those interviewed, 6.4 per cent said they felt their parents' influence at the age of five or younger, while 24.3 per cent said they began to feel it between the ages of six and nine. On top of that, 48 per cent of respondents felt that their parents strongly influenced their careers, with nearly 40 per cent saying they felt "heavily pressured" to follow their parents' input about their career paths (Joblist).

In my practice, this is something I come across a lot, particularly when working with younger clients. I work with ages 16 upward, and at times, 16- and 17-year-olds can be fraught with stress and anxiety about passing exams, choosing the "right" college courses and picking a field of study that their parents will approve of.

Research carried out in 2019 found that those from non-Western backgrounds had higher perceived parental career expectations than their Western-background peers, which had a significant effect on the former group's burnout (Griffin & Hu). So many of us from diverse cultural backgrounds joke about the pressure to go into law, medicine or finance, but when we seriously take stock, the burden to fill parental and family expectations can be intense. This pressure can make studying untenable. It can also lead to people taking out expensive loans for courses they never complete, going for interview after interview but not sticking to jobs, or pushing themselves to become more and more accomplished.

Sadly, I've seen clients breaking under the often unyielding pressures of living up to family expectations. This can lead to mental health difficulties, perfectionism, imposter syndrome, feelings of inadequacy, indecisiveness and apathy, due to people believing that nothing they do is ever good enough. These feelings can come wrapped up with a lot of guilt, which, although perfectly natural to experience from time to time, can carry a lot of weight. If left unchecked, this guilt can mushroom and develop into feelings of shame. I have seen clients wracked with guilt and shame around carer choices, friendships and relationships.

> **TOP TIP:** Breathe to let go
>
> If you are feeling guilty for prioritizing your own needs, take some time to journal on the matter that is making you feel guilty. Once you've finished, read back the overview. Then, try to be as neutral as possible as you

> write out a list of why it is important to do these things for your wellbeing.
>
> Read the list a few times and take some deep, cleansing breaths. As you consciously breathe out, imagine you are letting go of any negative emotion, tensions or guilt.
>
> You can mentally repeat phrases such as, "I release guilt", "I let go of self-doubt", "I choose my happiness", or anything else that resonates. With each exhalation, imagine any feelings of guilt disappearing from your body and mind.
>
> When you feel ready, return to your normal breathing, and take a few moments to assess how you feel.

STRATEGIES TO REFRAME FAMILIAL DISCONNECT

Although our communities can face various cross-cultural struggles, it is important to note that programming, patterns of behaviour and mindsets can shift and change. It's also important to remember that there are many opportunities for learning on both sides in a cross-cultural parent-child relationship. As I've highlighted, our parents have often grown up in a completely different sphere, with no blueprint on how to navigate an international, intergenerational family dynamic.

When I think back to when I was growing up, the media I saw that featured Black and brown families would rarely depict a happy story. I would see the positive and inspiring nuclear white family, while the family of colour's storylines would focus on poverty, terrorism, crime and danger. In the 1990s, 2000s and 2010s, how often did we see a happy immigrant family on TV, sharing love, being happy and living their best lives? Even now, despite positive progression and attempts at representation, it is still somewhat of a rarity. Of course, the perfect family does not exist, but it could be easy to look externally, see these glowing portrayals of white families, and perceive that other people (particularly your white peers) had it better growing up.

When reflecting on your family dynamic, try not to hold it up to Western standards. Despite a range of family styles existing around the world (same-sex parents, blended families, polygamous families, etc.), we are often taught that the model of two parents, two kids, a picket fence, a dog and a cat is the most optimal set up. In turn, we may subconsciously see this as the ideal, which can impact on how we make sense of our own family's cultural nuances.

> **REFLECTIVE MOMENT**
>
> Set a timer for at least 20 minutes. Then, journal on your childhood from your parents' perspective. What difficulties and challenges did they face? What was their upbringing like? What are the main differences between what they've been taught and what you've been taught?

Exercises such as this one are not set up to downplay childhood difficulties, but to look at the situation with an open mind, taking in all pieces of the puzzle. Whenever I consider the wider context of my parents' childhood, it helps me to hold any misunderstandings with more compassion and understanding.

For example, when I was in my early twenties, I would jump from job to job, to freelance and back again across a variety of industries. This was something that my mum, at times, found difficult to comprehend. Although she worked many jobs simultaneously, she believed in the value of a "trade", and worked very hard to build security for me and my siblings. Although, at times, we would disagree, looking back I can see that she was trying to guide me away from difficulties she'd experienced in her younger years around stability and security.

> **REFLECTIVE MOMENT**
>
> Take a moment to consider what your ideal relationship with your parents would be like, and then consider if it is realistic. What would it mean if they could not fulfil all the needs you want them to?

When working to release burdensome elements of our cultural backgrounds, it's important to note that many of our cultural norms have been imposed on us through the process of colonialization. For example, early European colonizers and kidnappers created a narrative around indigenous communities, casting them as "primitive", "uneducated", "sexually promiscuous" and "sexually heightened". These pressures placed intense strain on global-majority communities in so many ways – from formal Western education and homophobia, to the restriction of sexual freedom and shame around nudity.

Often, we feel as if we are going against our culture, but in reality, we are holding onto the shame of colonizers who transferred their own dishonour upon us. If you take time to investigate the history of your native land, you will often find that the traits your family or wider community are condemning may not actually be tied to your culture at all. Instead, they may just be a shambolic amalgamation of oppressive beliefs and colonial suppression.

I grew up in a working-class household. My parents were amazing role models in terms of work ethic, education and cultural capital. However, I did not grow up with an awareness around wealth building and financial literacy. When I graduated from university, I would listen to friends from wealthier backgrounds talk about the internships they had lined up, the deposits they would be gifted or the gap years they were due to take. On occasion, I would feel slighted by that. I would ask myself why I didn't have that experience and question whether I deserved it. As time moved on, I learned to focus on the positive values that my upbringing gifted me and sought out resources that could provide me with the financial education that I desired.

Sometimes, we place a high level of responsibility on our parents to meet all our childhood and adult child needs. No one person can meet all our needs. We accept this with our friends and partners, yet we can find it difficult to accept that about our primary carers. We can hold them to such high standards, but our parents are fallible, messy, neurotic humans, just like the rest of us.

> **REFLECTIVE MOMENT**
>
> Take some time to consider your parents'/primary caregivers' love language. How do they show love, and is it the same way you do?
>
> Perhaps they let you live at home rent-free. Perhaps they make sure you've got cooked meals and laundered clothes. Perhaps they maintain your car.
>
> These things might not seem as obvious as the style of love we are used to seeing in modern media, but they are expressions of love, nevertheless.

Once you have analysed your family's love language, it will be easier to consider how you can receive their style of love with the intention it is given. You can also use this to think about how you can show love differently. Perhaps after allowing a parent to cook for you, you do the dishes. This might seem standard, but if your parent's love language is acts of service, this could be a special and enriching experience for you both.

Along with thinking about how you can reframe your familial relationships, just like Mikey from the case study on page 72, there may be times when you need to figure out your boundaries and stand firmly in your own life choices. Our decisions will not always make our parents happy, and we must learn to live with that. As much as we may love or respect our parents, it is not our job to make them happy. Even if we have been raised to believe that what our parents or elders say is the be-all and end-all, as we mature, we need to develop or own thoughts and views, and make our own judgements.

Even as adults, we can seek our parents' validation, and it can feel very painful when they don't agree with something we are doing. However, if there are choices that we are making that are important to us, we need to learn to validate our own decisions. Remember, you are an adult, and you can validate yourself.

We often seek validation from people who would never do what we are doing. For example, if your parents are against your chosen career, please stop expecting them to support it. Instead, big yourself up and surround yourself with others who believe in your vocation.

When you are making a life decision, try your best not to base it on what your parents would think. You do not need to be the "good girl" or the "good boy". You are good enough in your own right, and others' opinions of you are not facts – they are simply judgements that are highly subjective.

If you can, try and live from a place of authenticity, and if it is safe to do so, try to avoid lying about what you are up to. There is a difference between choosing not to talk about your path and going out of your way to be dishonest. Untruthfulness can take us back to the mentality of not being good enough and continue a parent-young child dynamic, instead of creating an adult-to-adult connection.

Good communication is key when building stronger bonds. You can gain the support of a therapist or coach who will help you work out which boundaries are missing and how to create them. For example, if you enjoy spending time with your parents but don't want to be drawn into their disagreements, this would be an area where limits need to be set.

> **TOP TIP: Compromise comfortably**
>
> When working to create a boundary, consider ways in which you can compromise in a way that feels comfortable to you. For example:
>
> **Parent/carer:** I want you to text me when you arrive, let me know what time you will be home and then call me on the way home.
>
> **Adult child:** I will send you a text message to let you know I'm leaving and again to let you know I'm home safely. However, I do not want you to comment on how late it is, otherwise I will no longer be able to message you when I go out.

These conversations can seem frightening and will take some adjustment, but ultimately, we cannot get mad at people for flouting boundaries that we have not actually set. When working toward creating stronger emotional ties, it is important to not only focus on the negatives. Think about elements of family time that you enjoy, such as watching shows, listening to music, going to a place of worship or cooking together. Explore how you can factor that in with some regularity.

Once you start implementing these tweaks, you can take moments to reflect on how things go as they progress. There will be ups, downs, teething problems and everything in between, but that is normal. All changes take time. Know that this is a continuous journey and your parents are fallible, as are you. Reminding yourself of this when things get tough can provide a powerful prompt. Even if parents and family members don't always respond in the way you'd like, it's key to empower yourself by knowing that you are in control of your own behaviour and mindset. Regardless of other decisions, you can continue to work on yourself to change current and future family dynamics.

THE POSITIVE POWER OF CULTURAL DIVERSITY

When working toward internal integration, it is important to think about the positive aspects of being brought up among varied cultures. Third culture kids (TCK) are those raised in a culture other than their parents, while adult third culture kids (ATCK) do the same and continue living that culture beyond their childhood years. Having lived in both the UK and the Netherlands during my formative years – neither of which are my parents' countries of origin – I am an ATCK.

Many ATCKs I have worked with have shared that their unique childhoods have broadened their experience of the world. There are several benefits of being exposed to various cultural identities. In my work, I've found TCKs to have a rich understanding of the world, to be incredibly culturally competent, with sensitivity, compassion and thoughtfulness toward other worldviews.

Migrant children also have a higher level of adaptability, especially if they moved around a lot during their formative years. If you moved around during your childhood, you'd have already done more in your short life than many adults. That is not something to take lightly! This means that you'll have the skills to adapt to different groups of people, but also that you can communicate across cultural and national lines.

You will also have such a rich legacy from which to draw. Sometimes I liken the immigrant experience to having a blank canvas and a wide range of paint colours with which to decorate it. There is potential to create something unique and beautiful, but with no blueprint, it can be difficult to know where to start. When figuring out what your identity means to you, it's important to establish your core values, and figure out how similar or different they are to those within your family and cultural dynamic.

> **REFLECTIVE MOMENT**
>
> Create a list of 7–10 of your core values. These are the things that fundamentally guide your behaviour, decision making and actions, acting as a moral compass. (If you need some help to get you started, you can search online for a sample list.) Notice which ones resonate the most.
>
> Once you've written them down, put them in priority order and write a few sentences about what each one means to you and how you live it out.
>
> Then, do the same thing for your family members. You can create one for your entire immediate family, or separate it out into people of influence and their core values.
>
> Once you have all of your lists completed, line them up and reflect on any overlap or differences. What do they tell you about what values you have inherited and who you are now?

Often, when people do these exercises, it begins to illuminate key areas on which they would like to focus. For example, on my father's side of the family, both of my grandparents were pastors, and as such, religion and church attendance were both big parts of the value system. However, as an adult, I am not a Christian and identify as spiritual, so my life choices reflect who I am now and not this particular value I was raised with. On the other hand, there are values, such as being of service and giving back, which have been firmly embedded since I was a child. These values still resonate, and as a result, they have informed my chosen career, hobbies and voluntary endeavours.

So, when establishing the core values we want to live by, we can make the necessary changes needed to create a life and cultural identity that serves us.

CASE STUDY: Living in alignment

Merwa is a Sudanese born woman in her twenties. Merwa and her brother were raised in a single-parent household in Manchester. Merwa's mother had fled South Sudan following a tumultuous relationship with her husband and started life from scratch in the UK.

Merwa's mother was a very hard-working, practical person, and due to her life experience of having to be financially independent, she was heavily focused on building security. She encouraged Merwa and her brother to pursue medical careers and would often speak of them sending money back home once they had graduated.

> Merwa did not want to be a medical doctor – she was passionate about social care and wanted to become a counsellor. Merwa's mother had real difficulty accepting this. She felt that Merwa's interests were frivolous, and that social care was a poorly paid industry with no real prospects.
>
> Although Merwa did pursue a career in social care, she began to overwork herself as soon as she got her first role. Much of her social life disappeared, and she was constantly chasing the next promotion. When Merwa came to see me, she was burnt out and lacking in confidence.
>
> When we unpacked her value system, it was clear that she was living a life in line with her mother's cultural ideals and not her own. She was battling to prove to her mother that social care was a "real" career.
>
> I supported Merwa in creating a healthier work-life balance while also ensuring that she had the financial and structural stability she needed (a core value she *did* share with her mother).

Like Merwa, once we know which parts of our geographic and family cultures we would like to take forward, creating boundaries and building our own identities becomes an easier and less painful process.

If incorporating elements of your cultural upbringing has proved difficult, I would encourage you to take some time to complete the values exercise outlined on page 83 to figure out what's really important to you. Personal and cultural identities are complex, but by delving deeper and making intentional choices about who you want to be, you can navigate the journey more smoothly.

TAKE CARE TAKEAWAYS

- Feeling split between the culture you live in and your culture of origin is common and normal.
- Inter-group marginalization, aka being rejected from your culture of origin, can result in feelings of guilt and shame, and a split identity.
- Emotional difficulties between parent and child, as well as issues in connecting with each other, are both common parts of the migrant experience.
    - This can happen when children of different genders have different experiences, or through emotional distance or disagreements in career and academic choices.
- Exploring your parents' style of love, creating boundaries and finding common ground can help to create more understanding and better bonds.
- Validating yourself and your choices is a must.
- Examining your own personal values can reduce intercultural internal conflict.

4

COPING WITH COLOURISM

THE HISTORY OF COLOURISM

Colourism is happening within our communities, whether we notice it or not. At times, it is brazenly mentioned, and other times, it's stealthily unspoken. I am of a lighter brown skin tone, although I'm very clearly a Black woman, and over the years, I have been called names such as "lighty", "clear skinned", "lighted skinned" and "high yellow", both as compliments and insults.

The Oxford English Dictionary defines colourism as "prejudice or discrimination against individuals who have a dark skin tone, especially among people of the same ethnic or racial background."

I would say that is a fairly accurate description, and while colourism is not the same as racism, it is deeply rooted within it. Colourism is one of the most sinister reminders of a colonial past, and to this day, we are fed the message that physical attractiveness is synonymous with European features. Unfortunately, this belief of "light being right" is found within many cultures across the BIPOC diaspora, and it is extremely destructive.

To put it into context, colourism can be linked to culture and tradition within the Indian Caste system, which differentiates members of the community through class, region, religion, tribe, gender and language. The system assigns "high-caste" individuals to positive traits, such as wisdom and intelligence, while attributing the qualities of immorality and impurity to "low-caste" individuals (Deshpande).

The Dalits, the name of those who belong to the lowest caste, are known as the "untouchables" and have a darker skin tone. Although the caste system is much more complex and nuanced than focusing simply on skin colour, caste bias and colourism go hand in hand.

We can also see this in other parts of Asia, where colourism creates a divide between people of colour with indigenous physical attributes and those with Eurocentric features, or those who are deemed closer to whiteness. Fair skin is conflated with being upper class, while darker skin is associated with the opposite. As a result, those with a lighter skin tone are often revered. For example, billboards across Southeast and East Asia are filled with white-skinned models, despite inhabitants of these countries having a varied range of skin complexions.

We also see colourism within the Arab world, a diverse set of nations that host a range of religions, cultures, languages and ethnicities. Although there is not a caste system within the Middle East, there is a long-standing history of darker-skinned or African Arabs being seen as lesser than, with a cultural preference for

Eurocentric features, including white skin, straight hair and light eyes.

Modern slavery and the exploitation of cheaper labour is sadly still prevalent and often affects workers with darker complexions. In the Middle East, workers from African countries have been employed in conditions akin to slavery, performing strenuous manual labour with minimal pay. These workers face abuse, discrimination and legal vulnerability, which gives employers significant control of their workers' personal and social lives. Similar situations can also be found in Southeast Asia, the US, Canada, Australia and the EU. These entrenched systems perpetuate colourism by reinforcing social hierarchies wherein those with lighter skin are at the top.

The term *abd/abeed/abid* is an Arabic word meaning "slave" and is still unfortunately used as an ethnic slur for darker-skinned and Black Arabs. In 2018, campaigners on Twitter fought to remove usage of the word among the Arab community (Darwish).

I recall going out for the night years ago with a friend in a predominantly Arab part of London. My friend is of mixed Nubian-Arab-Egyptian heritage and has darker-toned skin. As we sat down to eat, she accidentally bumped into the chair of a man next to us who was talking loudly in Arabic to his friends. He was clearly insulted and proceeded to shout at the top of his voice:

"Watch where you're going, you Black bitch!"

We were 15 at the time and absolutely shocked that a grown man would behave in such a way. My friend, who was a particularly assertive young woman, replied, "I'm Arab like you, so if I'm a Black bitch, then so is your mother!"

Of course, my friend knew nothing about this man's mother, but her sentiment was strong – she was highlighting the fact that when two people from the same country display colourism, they're in fact destroying the culture from within. This was the first time I had seen colourism play out in an ethnic group other than my own, and I was bitterly disappointed to find out that it was something that spanned the globe.

Colourism has also made its way through the Black African diaspora globally, and there have been numerous studies analysing the variances in life outcomes of Black people depending on their skin tones. It has been found that darker-skinned females are three times more likely to be suspended from school than Black people with lighter skin tones (Hannon et al.). Studies into skin complexion and wages have also found that, shockingly, the disparity between darker-skinned and lighter-skinned African Americans echo differences we've seen between white and Black people (Goldsmith et al.). It has even been noted that having lighter Black skin leads to more lenient prison sentences, which is both scary and shocking (Viglione et al.).

When looking at members of the African diaspora within the Latino community, unfortunately, there have been similar findings. In a 2021 survey, 62 per cent of Hispanic adult respondents said that having a darker skin tone hurts their ability to get ahead, while a similar proportion said having a lighter skin colour helps. This study also found that, overall, darker-skinned Latinos were more likely to experience microaggressions and discrimination than lighter-skinned Latinos. And similarly to African Americans, it has been noted that Latinos and Afro-Caribbeans with darker skin and/or indigenous heritage consistently have less access to educational attainment, both in the form of basic literacy and university education (Pew Research Center).

> ## CASE STUDY: Rejection in the mother country
>
> Sammie is of mixed Dominican and Afro-Guyanese descent, and she felt rejected after visiting her mother's hometown in the Dominican Republic for the first time. She described feeling ignored and overlooked, while her lighter-skinned sibling was revered, respected and admired.
>
> She also experienced discomfort when hearing a number of derogatory slurs directed to the Dominican Republic's neighbouring nation, Haiti, and their often darker-skinned inhabitants.
>
> During her month-long stay, she spent much of her time indoors to avoid both tanning and swathes of colourist discrimination. It took her many years of reframing the colourist messaging to begin to love her brown skin again.

Unfortunately, stories like this are not uncommon, and many people who have Afro-Latino heritage experience discrimination and erasure with modern media, which only serves to reinforce the narrative that Latinos, Hispanics and South Americans are white, light-skinned or of mixed heritage. We can even see examples in reality TV shows like *Love and Hip Hop* and *Black Ink Crew*, where non-Afro Latino cast members use racial language and derogatory slurs when speaking to or about their Afro-Latinx and African American co-stars. This happens despite estimates that more than 90 per cent of enslaved Africans were sent to either Spanish or Portuguese colonies, which means that, today, Brazil houses the largest African diaspora in the world (Rahman).

Colourism has a long and complex history – colonial rule and the transatlantic slave trade have a big part to play in how pervasive it has become. During the mass enslavement of Africans, plantation owners would categorize the slaves they "owned" into two categories – house slaves (often children of slave owners and their mothers), and field slaves. House slaves lived and worked in the enslaver's main house, whereas field slaves lived outside in shacks with little protection from the elements. Of course, as with any unethical division of labour, this hierarchy created tensions among the communities of enslaved people. This led to a very stark and severe division between the darker-skinned field slaves and the lighter-skinned house slaves, which slave owners used to their advantage by pitting the two against one another.

For some communities, the idea of colourism pre-dates colonial rule. In East and Southeast Asian countries, the common notion during feudal times was that those who were able to live a life of leisure indoors stayed pale, while those who worked outdoors within farming communities were more tanned, so lighter skin became associated with the assumption that someone was better off financially. As time passed, ancient perceptions of skin colour became conflated with colonial racialized hierarchies, which only compounded ideals about lighter skin being more desirable.

Earlier, I spoke of the caste system in India, which, although connected, pre-dates colourism. During the British rule of the Indian subcontinent from 1858–1947, the British sustained the caste system in a very raw form, simply dividing people by skin colour, categorizing Europeans and white skin at the top of the grading (Rahman).

Of course, these historical events are much more comprehensive and impactful than I can discuss in a short chapter, but what these occurrences highlight is that these divisions by skin colour have ramifications even to this day.

CASE STUDY: Being both too dark and too light

Hema is British born with Indian Gujarati heritage, and she struggled with the imagery of the "ideal woman" throughout her childhood and adolescence.

She described growing up in a rural part of the UK with limited access to other people of colour. At school, she felt unattractive because she did not fit in with the popular blond hair, blue eyes aesthetic she saw in the mass media. At the same time, when she was around her extended family, she would often have her fair skin tone and features compared to those of the often lighter-eyed and -skinned actors in Bollywood movies.

A particularly poignant moment for her was when her parents told her that she'd have no problem finding a husband due to the fairness of her skin. This juxtaposition of being both "too dark" in school and "too light" among

> her family caused Hema to feel conflicting emotions – she felt lucky to be lighter-skinned and also unlucky to be born brown at all.
>
> I worked with Hema to deconstruct these harmful narratives. She now feels proud of her heritage and physical appearance as a part of her, but not simply because of the shade of her skin.

Colourism is also heavily linked to anti-Blackness, which is a very specific type of racial discrimination. All forms of racism and discrimination are unacceptable, but it's important to be aware of the different distinctions that can exist within culturally diverse communities – for example, Islamophobia, anti-Semitism and, of course, anti-Blackness.

Anti-Blackness is the exclusion of individuals who are (or are perceived to be) of Black African descent. Black history is tragically unique due to the transatlantic slave trade, and this has resulted in the othering of Black people – even within the BIPOC community. This can show up in practice through the preservation of anti-Black narratives, such as children of colour being told they're not allowed to date a Black person, or the perpetual view that Black people are lazy, uneducated or dangerous.

In the 1940s, husband-and-wife psychologists Kenneth and Mamie Clark conducted a study on the effects of segregation using four dolls. By asking children to choose which dolls they preferred and why, they found that both white and Black children assigned positive characteristics to the white doll, creating a sense of inferiority among the Black children (Beschloss). This study has been replicated in many ways throughout the years, but sadly, the results continually show negative perceptions of Blackness. After years of being drip-fed harmful messaging, anti-Blackness is still very much a part of our collective psyche.

A quick Google search will show you that there are numerous racial slurs for Black people that exist, hailing from all corners of the world – South Africa, the US, UK, Brazil and more. Of course, there are multiple variations of the N-word, too.

Anti-Blackness has led to Black body characteristics being perceived as unattractive – unless they appear on a white person! For example, many Black people have grown up being teased for their hair and physical features and facing negative consequences for simply existing in their Black bodies. However, celebrities who are not Black, such as Kim Kardashian, receive praise for having large butts, pumping up their lips and flaunting braids.

Circumstances like these continuously reinforce to both Black and non-Black people that Blackness is not acceptable *unless* it is partnered or preceded with whiteness. On top of this, Black people who appear to have assimilated into white culture are seen as "better", which can further force Black people to hide elements of their Blackness to try and avoid oppressive and outdated anti-Black views.

In 2020, like most of the world, I watched a plethora of TV series, including one called *Indian Matchmaking*, which saw marriage consultant Sima Taparia attempt to match singles with prospective brides and grooms. The show was a difficult watch, as it had a large focus on potential candidates being "fair" (light-skinned). This was seen as a positive attribute, particularly for women. Later that year,

South Asian dating service Shaadi.com was taken to task for allowing singles to filter potential dates by skin tone on their website (Bilikhu). These instances shone a light into the darkest corners of colourist and anti-Black dating preferences.

Growing up, I witnessed many incidents like these. As mentioned at the start of the chapter, I was simultaneously revered and insulted for my lighter skin tone. There were several songs released during the noughties that hailed "lighties" as being the ones to date, and as a result, I'd often get guys interested in talking to me just because I was a "lighty". On the other hand, I'd often get disrespected for my light skin, with people telling me I thought I was "too nice because I'm light-skinned". So, I would feel a mixture of guilt for my light skin, relief to be light-skinned and anguish at the focus on my skin colour at all. It was a very confusing time, and one that deeply impacted my relationship with my sense of self. Even now, there are still grown adults (usually men) who've told me they are mainly (or only!) attracted to light-skinned and mixed women. For me, this is a *major* red flag!

> ### REFLECTIVE MOMENT
>
> When thinking about your dating preferences, consider whether colourism or anti-Blackness has played a part in who you find attractive.
>
> If you've noticed you have a type, delve deeper into where that comes from and examine whether any of your perceptions need challenging.

Another element of colourism and anti-Blackness is texturism – discrimination against those with a coarse, thicker or denser hair type (e.g., an afro). This has played out in my life, too, as my slightly curlier-than-average afro often gets described as "good hair", due to its similarity to a Eurocentric curl pattern.

Texturism has led to hair discrimination, or the unfair treatment of people based on their hair's natural characteristics. This has played out in workplace and school policies that prohibit hair styles commonly worn by those of African descent, such as braids, locs and cornrows. These policies solely impact people of colour and perpetuate harmful narratives about Black hair being sloppy and unkempt.

In the US, there are a series of state municipal laws known as the CROWN Act – "Creating a Respectful and Open World for Natural Hair" – which disallow discrimination based on hair styles and textures. While there have been global efforts by activists and policymakers to address hair discrimination, specific laws like the CROWN Act do not exist in many countries. Without these protections in place, it's even more important to continue to challenge colourism, texturism, anti-Blackness and hair discrimination.

These "the closer to white, the better" storylines have been passed down from generation to generation. I remember talking with a friend of mine whose heritage is Punjabi Indian about going back home for the summer holidays, and we realized we had something in common: our grandparents did not want us to sunbathe because they didn't want us to tan. Although these views might seem backwards, our ancestors were not stupid – they were people in vulnerable positions who had been brainwashed for generations in very deliberate ways by calculating colonialists.

So, as we can see, due to the issues with colourism and anti-Blackness, unfortunately, there is still a level of social capital that many refer to as "light-skinned privilege". This is not to say that people of colour with a lighter skin tone do not experience racism, discrimination and prejudice. However, they may hold a level of privilege based on having a skin tone perceived by society as more desirable, especially compared to those with darker skin. Light-skinned privilege can also refer to people of colour who are sometimes described as "white passing", which means they are perceived as white due to their features and/or skin tone. This term is problematic and offensive – firstly, because it implies that these individuals are trying to "pass" under the radar; secondly, because it places whiteness as the standard; and thirdly, because race and ethnicity are about so much more than physical appearance. Unfortunately, we still live in a world that categorizes people in this arbitrary way.

People who present as white might experience a level of privilege, as they may be able to move around in majority-white spaces with a level of anonymity. They may also be able to choose whether to disclose that they are a person of colour. I remember working with an old colleague who was of mixed heritage, but often mistaken for being Caucasian. He described it as his "superpower" and enjoyed being able to blend into a variety of white spaces without having to highlight his difference.

However, for many white-presenting people of colour, there can be double discrimination, as they may face prejudice within both white and BIPOC spaces. This can be compounded if people feel that they cannot "place" a white-presenting person of colour – for example, if someone they perceive to be white has a non-white-sounding name. There are also incidents where white-presenting individuals can experience higher levels of racism, as people do not identify them as a person of colour, either.

An incident that springs to mind comes from a client of mine who was racially traumatized when spending time with a group of white colleagues who made racial slurs about South Asians, not realizing that she was of mixed South Asian and Italian heritage. The incident caused her great distress, and she could not believe how freely her colleagues used racist language in front of one another.

As we can see, it's important to realize that, although there are privileges associated with lighter skin tones, there are still universal and unique difficulties that all people of colour face. That is why it is so important for us to work together and to dismantle these toxic colourist narratives.

HOW TO LOVE THE SKIN YOU'RE IN

Colourism plays a large role in how young people of colour make sense of themselves and where they belong in the world. This is not helped by modern music, media and film, as colourism has plagued the big screen and music industry for many years.

Movies and TV have a major impact on societal norms, values and beliefs, and sadly, both can propagate harmful narratives. As people of colour, we have found our way onto Hollywood screens, but we have often had to deal with characters portraying our communities and the people within them in stereotypical ways. For example, common on-screen tropes include "the loud Black best friend", "the Black male thug", "the Arab terrorist" or the "the dorky academic Asian". These stereotypical characters then layer on top of colourist casting, meaning that BIPOC representation is still subpar. When we look at Hollywood, Bollywood, Nollywood, the Anime scene and more, we can see a culture of colourism running throughout them all.

For example, the films generated by India's Bollywood industry have mostly featured leading actors with paler skin and anglicized features that do not provide representation for many people of Indian heritage. Within Bollywood, language has also played a big part, with words used such as *kaalu/kali/kala*, which are all derogatory terms for being dark-skinned, and *goriya*, which was originally the name of a Hindu caste but is now often used as a term for a fair-skinned lady.

Alongside their often light-skinned leads, Bollywood films tend to use dark-skinned actors to depict villains – characters of varying ethnicities serve as evil "baddies" among a sea of paler-skinned "goodies". We've also seen several artists being "blackened up" to depict a less desirable character or darker-skinned character. This happens in both Bollywood *and* Hollywood. For example, in 2016, Bollywood actor Alia Bhatt played the role of an immigrant farmer in the film *Udta Punjab*, and Zoe Saldana played the role of prolific singer-songwriter Nina Simone. This highlights both negative attitudes toward dark skin and the resistance to hiring darker-skinned actors to play the roles of dark-skinned characters.

Colourism is also rife within the music industry, with light-skinned women dominating the music charts. When you think of the most famous women of colour in the music world, you probably see Beyonce, Alicia Keys, Rihanna, Nicki Minaj or Mariah Carey. There are a wide range of talented women from all backgrounds and of all shades, but we are consistently shown the image of the light-skinned, sultry RnB starlet.

When we look at the UK, things are not much different. I struggle to think of even five darker-skinned musicians that I've seen with vast commercial success within my lifetime. It's not just mainstream Western music that has this problem – we've seen similar issues in genres such as K-pop, which has had numerous complaints of colourism over the years.

> **REFLECTIVE MOMENT**
>
> Think back to your childhood memories of TV, music and film.
> Which characters and famous stars did you most resonate with, and why?
> Which characters and famous stars did you dislike, and why?

As a person of colour, it's nearly impossible to swerve the impact of colourism. We are constantly and subliminally told that lighter skin is more beautiful. Like the media industry, the advertising and beauty industries consistently hail European beauty standards as the pinnacle. Many of us have been seeing these images from a very young age, and studies carried out in both the UK and Africa have found that adolescents of colour often express a desire for lighter skin tones and/or are dissatisfied with their skin tones because of this subliminal messaging (Craddock et al.).

When we look at other areas of the world, we can see similar results. A study conducted in East Asia found that nearly half of Chinese and Taiwanese people, and more than a quarter of Japanese and Korean people, had used skin-lightening products (Glenn).

It has also been noted that before the summer of 2020, only 13 per cent of ads within the United States featured darker-skinned models. Following the resurgence of the BLM movement, this rose to almost 25 per cent in June 2020, but by August 2020, that figure had dropped back down to 16 per cent (Mallick). It seems that darker skin was only a passing trend because anti-racism and BLM were in vogue.

Sadly, this media's preference for lighter skin commonly results in the usage of products designed to bleach, lighten or whiten skin. In 2020, the skin-bleaching market was valued at US $8.6 billion, or roughly £6.5 billion (Hall). Sadly, these products are often endorsed by celebrities in ads that target younger and more impressionable audiences.

In 2020, global beauty brand Unilever was called to account, as their products were seen to perpetuate colourism. Fair & Lovely – one of their well-known skin creams sold in India, Bangladesh, Thailand, Sri Lanka, Malaysia and other parts of Asia – had its name changed to Glow & Lovely. Unilever also removed the words "fair/

fairness", "white/whitening" and "light/lightening" from their product packs and communication (Unilever). I dread to think how many young people had been influenced by the wording on the box – in both the product's name and description – before this very recent change.

This messaging has such a detrimental impact on our communities and us as individuals. We are all subconsciously absorbing racist and colourist messaging, and many of us will experience internalized racism at some point in our lives. Internalized racism can play out in the form of holding negative views about ourselves and those with darker skin. These harmful self-assessments can create a desire to change one's physical appearance, with the subconscious or conscious focus on changing "visibly ethnic" features. This doesn't only manifest through skin lightening – it can also be done through hair dyeing, hair straightening, plastic surgery or the removal of body hair.

CASE STUDY: Growing up with dark skin in the UK

Aanchal is a British-born woman of South Indian heritage. She grew up as a dark-skinned woman in a multicultural South London borough. During her teenage years in the 1990s, she described feeling "wholly unattractive". When spending time with her cousins, she was viewed as "too dark", "too hairy" and having "too many curls".

For many years Aanchal tried furiously to change her physical appearance by straightening her hair, dyeing it

> from black to brown, avoiding the sun and removing as much of her body hair as possible.
>
> It was during the 2020 lockdown when she didn't have access to salons that she was forced to embrace her natural beauty in a way she hadn't before.
>
> Through this process, Aanchal grew to a space of comfort with her features, and when lockdown lifted, she decided to keep her natural curls, hair colour and to reduce her hair removal routine.

Now, please don't get me wrong – enjoying beauty treatments in and of itself does not signify that someone has internalized self-hatred. These are just some examples of how colourism and colonial pressures can play out.

If you indulge in beauty procedures that aim to change core aspects of your cultural features, I'd encourage you to think a little bit deeper about what you choose to do and why.

When I graduated from university, I had my own journey with my features to overcome. At the time, I had a massive afro, and as much as I loved it, I would often hear comments such as, "You're so brave," "Will you straighten it when you get a job?" and, "What will you do with your hair when you get married?"

As a result, whenever I had a job interview, I would make sure that my hair was as flat as possible – I would usually opt for braids over my free-flowing afro to maintain a level of "professionalism". My perception around this since changed, of course. I know that all hair types are beautiful and suitable for a professional environment. I now wear my hair in its natural form with pride, regardless of the occasion.

> **REFLECTIVE MOMENT**
>
> **Think of your beauty and self-care routine.**
> **Have you ever felt the need to modify any of your natural features to "fit in"?**
> **What can you do to work toward embracing those features now?**

Even though colourism may seem like a purely social or political issue, there is something about our connection with our skin that is deeply spiritual. The skin is our largest organ and a portal for connection, stimulation of hormones and even temperature regulation. The condition of our skin can reflect our physical, emotional and psychological health. Plus, our skin is a connector between our physiological internal and external worlds. So, if we receive negative messaging about our skin, then there can be a range of effects on our overall wellbeing.

I sometimes see this when clients subconsciously disengage from their skin, perhaps rushing to get dressed after a shower, not wanting to touch it or choosing not to look in the mirror. For me, I see connecting with our skin as a way for people of colour to reclaim our roots and pay homage to the skin's native journey.

TOP TIP: Soothe with self-touch and celebrate your skin

1. **Give yourself a hug.** Sit comfortably, wrap both arms around your torso and give yourself a big squeeze. Doing this can stimulate the same sensations as if another person was hugging you, boosting both oxytocin and serotonin levels. This is a beautiful practice to soothe, calm anxiety and send your body and skin some love.
2. **Place your hands on your heart/abdomen.** While seated, place your hands on your body, feel the rise and fall of your chest and stomach as you breath, and tune in to the sensation of your skin underneath your hands. Breathing deeply into these areas can help activate the parasympathetic branch of the nervous system, allowing you to relax, rest and restore.
3. **Give yourself a massage.** Self-massage is a big part of many indigenous cultures – African diasporic creaming of the body and scalp, Indian head massage and Ayurvedic Abhyanga are all ways in which self-touch has been used across our communities. Choose your oil of choice (e.g., cocoa butter, coconut oil or sesame oil), find a quiet and warm space, and give yourself a full body massage, starting from the head and face and working your way down to the toes. Enjoy the sensation of pampering your skin and giving it the love it so truly deserves.

These three tips are just a starter. If you get creative, there will be many ways you can think of to celebrate and luxuriate in your skin. In my case, during a period of particularly bad allergies, I discovered self-administered facial lymphatic drainage on YouTube, and now I love taking time out to give myself a mini-facial and treatment at the end of a long day. I do the same with self-reflexology on my feet. These practices not only form a part of my self-care, but they reaffirm to myself that my body and skin are worthy and deserving of love and nurture.

Feeling comfortable in your skin can look different for everyone but it can be extremely empowering to reach a place of acceptance, tenderness and love for the skin you've been blessed with. This does not mean feeling confident every single moment of every day, nor does it mean believing you are "perfect". It simply means appreciating your natural qualities without seeking "perfection" or feeling "lesser than".

If you find yourself looking at Western beauty standards as comparison, take care to examine your internal dialogue and challenge media that perpetuates harmful beauty standards. Change the discourse from, "Why don't I look like that?" to, "Why am I only seeing one image of beauty?" If you struggle to talk to yourself in a loving way, consider how you would speak to a loved one – would you ever berate them the way you berate yourself?

There is absolutely no evidence that having lighter, whiter skin or anglicized features makes people happy. There is no perfect appearance formula for happiness. I work with a plethora of clients every day, and physical characteristics play little bearing on whether someone is truly happy. Peace, contentment and joy are only ever an inside job.

REFLECTIVE MOMENT

A powerful way to reframe your thought process is to use affirmations that elicit a positive belief. Saying something positive about your body can be a powerful way to move forward on your anti-colourism journey.

Affirmations for skin love and acceptance can include:
- I love the skin I'm in.
- My skin is beautiful.
- My features are beautifully unique.
- I accept myself as I am.

You can also make them specific to your traits:
- I love the shape of my nose.
- My eyes are a beautiful shade of brown.
- My hair is thick and luscious

Using affirmations may seem counterintuitive at first but it's somewhat of a "fake it 'til you make it" mentality.

Writing affirmations in a journal, mentally repeating them during meditation or reciting them in the mirror can help reframe the stories we tell ourselves. It might feel awkward at first, but the more you repeat your affirmations, the easier it will get, and the more your subconscious mind will absorb these messages.

What other affirmations can you think of to celebrate, appreciate and embrace your features?

Unlearning the harmful lessons of colourism is a journey, and it can take time. Please know that even if you follow every single tip here to a tee, working toward self-acceptance in this way is an ongoing journey.

There will be times when you'll feel like the best thing since sliced bread, and there will be other days when the battle might feel too difficult. That is normal and to be accepted. Healing is not linear – there will be ups and downs. Be gentle with yourself. If you continue to do the work, you'll undoubtedly be moving toward a place of growth.

RESOURCES TO MOVE PAST COLOURISM

So, how do we move forward and start to heal from colourism? Well, firstly, we need to work toward reducing judgement of others based on the colour of their skin. This is easier said than done, as we all hold unconscious biases, but it is important to live from a place of awareness when these thought patterns inevitably come up.

For those who are lighter-skinned, think about how you can use your privilege to advocate for our darker-skinned brothers and sisters. We need to be courageous and address colourism within our communities. If you see it, call it out. Don't let not-so-innocent jokes pass by and challenge harmful statements about skin tone.

Have conversations about colourism within your families and communities where possible. Ask your parents, grandparents, siblings and cousins about their perspectives. Finding out what attitudes already exist can provide a great base to start from. Sometimes, approaches toward skin tone have been embedded within cultural and familial narratives for so long that no one ever thinks to question them, but change can only come with both discussion and action.

The workplace can be another environment where we hold influence for positive change. A few years back, I worked in the youth service and noticed that many of the psycho-social educational videos that were being shown to young people perpetuated racial and colourist stereotypes. During a training course on sexual violence in universities, the "educational" video we watched showed only dark-skinned Black and South Asian males as perpetrators of sexual violence, and white women as the victims. I was horrified at this implicit association between men of colour and sexual violence. I made a complaint to the course organizers, as did another delegate who was of South Asian heritage. Eventually, the video was removed from the course content.

These harmful narratives can be reproduced from an early age. I remember when my dear niece started secondary school and went into one of her first Personal, Social, Health and Economic education (PSHE) classes. On the introductory PowerPoint, she saw Black people and asked the teacher if they were learning about slavery. The teacher asked her how she knew that, and she replied that the only time she ever learned about Black people in school was when discussing slavery.

Her teacher was simultaneously shocked and enlightened to hear an 11-year-old make such an astute observation and, hopefully, he used her insight to work toward implementing changes to lesson plans. As sad as it is, my niece was right: our Black and brown children rarely see images of themselves in a positive light, and we, as the older generation, can work to change this.

> **TOP TIP:** Build confidence in the next generation
>
> It's important to raise those younger than us to move forward in a new way. With children and young people in our family and networks, we must support them to feel comfortable in their skin.
>
> When telling children that they're beautiful, try not to relate it to certain "desirable" features such as "long hair" or "fair skin".
>
> Show children pictures of relatives, ancestors and public figures who look like them with a diverse range of noses, lips, bodies, eye shapes and hair textures.

When considering our subliminal programming, it's important to be a conscious consumer and viewer. When on social media, I ensure to follow people, pages and brands that highlight the beauty of melanated skin and culturally diverse features.

For example, when I was a bridesmaid for a friend in 2021, I became stressed about the lack of bridal make-up available for my skin tone. I came across mainly white bloggers, West Africans with much darker skin tones or West Asian makeup artists with much lighter skin tones. A friend of mine suggested following South Asian beauty bloggers, and it completely changed my perception of what is out there for women of my skin tone. There are whole social movements now dedicated to different skin tones and hair types. For example, hashtags such as #NaturalHairCommunity, #MelaninPoppin and #BrownSkinGirl have been used to celebrate the versatility and beauty of natural afro hair and melanated skin. Tapping into these channels can kick-start a powerful process of skin and hair reclamation.

> **TOP TIP:** Follow the right people
>
> Diversify your social media feed. Find people of influence with a variety of skin tones that you can look up to, and unfollow any pages that make you feel bad about yourself.

> **TAKE CARE TAKEAWAYS**
>
> - Colourism and skin-tone preference are embedded within most BIPOC communities, stemming from colonial history and slavery.
> - Anti-Blackness and texturism play a big role in the perpetuation of negative stereotyping and colourist discrimination.
> - Mass media, TV and film have contributed to the ways in which we perceive both darker and lighter skin. If you've ever felt bad about your skin tone, it's not your fault!
> - The beauty and skin-lightening industries have a major impact on perpetuating the belief that lighter skin is more beautiful, but this is simply not true. We are all beautiful!

- Considering your own internal bias is a big part of unlearning colourism.
- Practising self-soothing techniques and positive affirmations can help to create a positive connection with your skin.
- Moving past colourism means raising children to see their beauty, diversifying your network and working toward a place of self-acceptance.

5

TRANSFORMING TRANSGENERATIONAL TRAUMA

SIGNS AND SYMPTOMS OF SECONDARY TRAUMA

When working in mental health and wellbeing, trauma is something that comes up a *lot*. The word "trauma" refers to an intensely distressing event that impacts on an individual's sense of emotional, psychological or spiritual wellbeing. It can be mild, moderate or severe, and can leave long-lasting effects on how a person thinks, feels and shows up in the world. Transgenerational trauma traces how these difficult events – and their effects on a person's sense of self – pass through generations.

My own personal history encompasses various levels of transgenerational trauma – my ancestors were European slave owners, enslaved Africans, displaced Indigenous Americans and targeted elders from the Windrush generation. Although I haven't personally experienced these incidents, the memories of them run through my genealogy, and I've heard the accounts numerous times. Listening to stories about enslavement or brutality against Indigenous Americans is enough to bring a tear to my eye, and it never gets easier to hear, despite how much I learn.

When we hear stories from others around us which are particularly traumatic, we can experience what's called secondary trauma (also sometimes known as vicarious trauma). Secondary trauma is a form of emotional or psychological distress that people are indirectly exposed to through hearing and/or witnessing the experience of others.

The thing that makes secondary trauma different to other types of traumas is that you don't experience the trauma yourself. Secondary trauma can include hearing a first-hand account of another's experience, viewing distressing images online or even looking after a person who is unwell. The latter type of trauma is often associated with people who work in healthcare, such as nurses, paramedics or doctors, but generally speaking, secondary trauma does not discriminate and can impact anyone. If someone is privy to another's traumatic history, they too can experience symptoms such as anxiety, flashbacks and extreme hypervigilance.

Along with psychological symptoms, secondary trauma can have a major impact on the mind and body. Emotional symptoms can include mistrust of others, grief, sadness, self-isolation and low mood. Physically, people can experience a host of unwanted issues, including headaches, fatigue, digestive issues and insomnia.

Mentally, it can cause a negative outlook, loss of hope, loss of purpose and intrusive thoughts. Parents and carers impacted by trauma may find it difficult to respond optimally during the usual ups and downs of life, or the developmental stages in their children's lives. They may become emotionally detached, numb or go on to develop serious mental health illness. This can impact children as they develop, as it may be hard for them to learn a healthy sense of interdependence and emotional regulation.

CASE STUDY: Secondary trauma in the family

Amir is a 21-year-old British-born man of Afghani heritage. His parents came to the UK in 1998, fleeing from the conflict in Afghanistan.

Amir's father experienced severe post-traumatic stress disorder following his experience in his home country. He would often experience flashbacks, extreme anxiety over loud noises, and flip between being calm and agitated. Sometimes, he would experience periods of low mood, which would leave him incapacitated and unable to get out of bed.

Amir, his mother and his younger sister were constantly on tenterhooks, and found it difficult to witness their father and husband jumping, shaking and sobbing due to his flashbacks and memories. Amir began to take on extra household responsibilities, such as childcare and housework. When his father was unwell, he would rush home from school to look after him.

> Amir's father would describe the world as a dangerous place and had a strong belief that war could break out at any moment. Amir began to internalize his father's fears and became anxious and fearful of the world around him, leading to a diagnosis of clinical anxiety.

Although secondary trauma is not specific to us as BIPOC people, many global-majority families have experienced a level of trauma due to racism, discrimination, displacement and structural injustice.

THE IMPACT OF SOCIAL MEDIA

In today's modern society, we are exposed to hundreds of images every day, and the constant stream of news, social media and traditional media can play a significant role in our mental health. For one thing, we easily come across distressing imagery online, whether we want to see it or not. This happens with increasing frequency and can lead to secondary trauma.

Although I want to keep updated with what is going on in the world, there are times when I simply cannot bear to log on to social media for fear of what horror I will see next. It has been noted in numerous studies that social media exposure of collective trauma is associated with worse mental health. Many accounts now show incredibly traumatic footage, whether they're purely reporting the news, trying to stoke activism or engaging in sensationalism for clicks. These videos can be deeply distressing. However, we often do not realize the compound impact that this can have. An example that comes to mind for me is the first six months of the pandemic. As a global community, we were constantly bombarded with fear-inducing images of illness and death, as well as police brutality and racist attacks on both Black people and members of the East Asian, Southeast Asian and Pacific Islander diaspora.

Although I did not witness those events with my own eyes, seeing them repeatedly via social media impacted me in a deeply emotive way. I struggled with sleepless nights, nightmares and anxiety related to the pandemic and police brutality. At the time of writing this book, I am witnessing the humanitarian crises unfolding in Palestine, Sudan and Ethiopia, among many others. The impact on my mental health has been palpable, and I have had to be extremely careful of what I consume to continue working, functioning and managing my own wellbeing.

During the pandemic and at other times, in an attempt to spread awareness, people shared extremely graphic imagery of Black and brown deaths, pain and torture. Although intentions for sharing this footage may have been good, doing so repeatedly only serves to desensitize us to POC pain and, in my opinion, does not contribute to empathy toward global-majority communities. There are many ways to provide support and allyship that do not involve the dishonour of Black and brown bodies, while simultaneously potentially traumatizing your followers and online friends.

TOP TIP: Cope with distressing imagery

If you see an image or video that has had a negative impact on you, the first thing you should do is close down the screen. Take a few deep breaths, and where possible, try to do some form of physical movement. This could be jogging on the spot, stretching or going for a walk.

Even if you see it through a screen, distressing imagery can create a physiological trauma response, flooding the body with stress hormones. Moving will support the body to release this, helping to break the cycle of fight or flight.

When it is time to return to your device, try to avoid looking at the image/re-watching the video, as repeated exposure of traumatic content puts you at risk of worsening symptoms.

TOP TIP: Clean up your feed

If you are someone who regularly uses social media or news apps, ponder on how well these platforms are serving you. Consider how often you check them and when. Reflect on how they make you feel and try some of the following tips:

Unfollow or unfriend. Remove any accounts that make you feel negative, anxious or fearful. This could be a news outlet that constantly scaremongers or a friend who reshares disturbing posts and stories. If you feel uncomfortable unfollowing people you know, then mute them or hide their content.

> **Cultivate your content.** Take time to follow accounts you find inspiring, positive and engaging for a more balanced feed. I have a specific social media account for following funny pages, dance pages and travel blogs.
>
> **Alter your notification settings.** Notifications create a spike in dopamine, but they can also cause anxiety. Consider turning off notifications so you can choose when to opt into social media.
>
> **Limit your social media usage.** Use your phone's settings to review the amount of time you spend on social media. Consider setting time limits through your phone or external app blockers to limit the time you spend online.
>
> **Hack the algorithm.** Social media algorithms show you more of what you engage with. By liking, commenting on, saving and sharing content you love, you'll end up seeing more of it.

The consequences of secondary trauma can be immediate, like it was for me during the pandemic. However, it can also impact people with delayed onset. I saw this quite often in my work as a mental health coach with clients not realizing the full impact of the pandemic until it was fully underway – or in some cases, until it was over!

TRANSGENERATIONAL TRAUMA

Another way trauma can be passed down through the generations is through transgenerational trauma, also known as intergenerational trauma. Unlike secondary trauma, this type of trauma is often unspoken and can impact individuals, families, communities or entire ethnic groups.

Transgenerational trauma arises when people are affected by major events, such as a natural disaster, humanitarian crisis, war, genocide or famine. Though the events may be long gone, the impact of the historical and ancestral trauma can live on through children, grandchildren and further generations.

Transgenerational trauma can be passed down through nurture, learned behaviours, family dynamics and socialization. The emerging field of epigenetics, which examines how a person's environment and behaviours can change the way their genes work, also highlights how transgenerational trauma can impact DNA function, with some studies finding correlations between prenatal and preconception trauma and gene alteration.

For example, there have been numerous studies carried out about transgenerational trauma in descendants of Holocaust survivors. These survivors went through hell and back, only to be relocated and then greeted with racism, hostility and antisemitism. It has now been found that their children and grandchildren show an increased vulnerability for stress, including higher cortisol levels (Dashorst et al.).

For those who, like me, are descendants of the transatlantic slave trade, the impacts can also be seen to this day. The slave trade spanned over 400 years, and the racial stigma toward Black people has been hard to shift. As such, it has been found that the intergenerational impact of the transatlantic slave trade can lead to feelings of low self-esteem, as well as psychological and behavioural impacts for descendants of Africans who were enslaved (Degruy).

Although the Holocaust and the slave trade are two of the most well-known and large-scale events that could cause transgenerational trauma, many communities within the global-majority diaspora have experienced cultural and historical events that impact descendants to this day – the partition of India, the expulsion of South Asians in East Africa, the Vietnam War, the genocide of indigenous people or the intergenerational effects of the occupation of Palestine, to name a few. There are too many examples to mention here, but this list already highlights how much of a risk for both secondary and intergenerational trauma our communities face.

CASE STUDY: Apartheid and transgenerational trauma

Johan is a 28-year-old South African-Dutch second-generation immigrant living in the UK. His father was born in the early 1950s and grew up during apartheid.

Being a Black African in South Africa at that time, Johan's father experienced segregation, severe racial discrimination, poverty and violence. He decided to leave South Africa in the early 1990s. He met his wife, from the Netherlands, and later had Johan and his siblings.

> The aftereffects of experiencing many years of trauma in his home country left Johan's father shell-shocked and withdrawn. Although he did not speak of his experiences often, Johan described being able to *feel* the energy of apartheid in the background during his childhood and young adult life.
>
> He described feelings of listlessness, hopelessness and shame about his mixed South African background. Johan worked with me to reframe some of these feelings. He also spoke to a traditional talking therapist to unpick some of the deeper feelings around his experience of intergenerational trauma.

Both secondary and transgenerational trauma can be difficult to spot, as the symptoms overlap with a range of other conditions. As you forge a path of self-awareness and healing, it is always important to reach out for support if symptoms are present. Breaking silence, releasing shame and sharing secrets can reduce the stigma associated with discussing the effects of historical and systemic trauma.

Although it may be difficult, as with much of the content in this book, the journey of healing is incredibly empowering. There's nothing quite like developing a sense of independence as you look back on how far you've come.

Seeking support through professional, self-help and holistic methods can help you to discover root causes, break cycles, learn coping strategies and generate powerful emotional, psychological wellbeing. The restorative journey is vital for severing the ties to the trauma that impacted the generations that came before us.

TURNING TRAUMA INTO GROWTH

Learning about all the ways in which our communities have been negatively impacted can feel overwhelming or even as if our communities are doomed. However, I like to frame it differently. In my eyes, knowledge is power, and by having an awareness of how these various issues may impact us, we can empower ourselves to approach them with strength, creativity and resilience.

Over the past few years, I have taken time to delve deeper into my own cultural history with visits to the US, the Caribbean and Africa, and through courses and self-study. I've been astounded by the power, knowledge and wisdom held by my ancestors.

An example I like to draw on is the theory of post-traumatic growth developed by psychologists Richard Tedeschi and Lawrence Calhoun in the 1990s. This term refers to the positive psychological changes that people may go through after experiencing a traumatic event.

It does not mean that every trauma will create growth, but it highlights the positive transformations that can occur in various people's lives following periods of hardship. Post-traumatic growth can give people a newfound sense of strength, perspective, resilience, focus, appreciation for life or spiritual connection.

Many of the world's greatest leaders and change-makers, such as Nelson Mandela, Malala Yousafzai and Oprah Winfrey, went through great trials before using their newfound insight for good. Now, I'm not saying you have to be the next Mandela, but it can be useful to think of experiences you've been through and analyse the learning. Often, you will realize there is a wisdom inside you that you can draw on in even the toughest of times.

As I mentioned earlier, I really struggled during the 2020 pandemic with secondary trauma due to global events. Initially, I survived by reducing my media consumption, but eventually I found a way to challenge my pain through creating poetry and anti-racism educational content. Although it was a very difficult time of my life, I truly believe that without that experience, I would not have written this book. Through adversity, I was able to develop my passion for racial justice and BIPOC wellbeing, and I am grateful for the learning.

> **REFLECTIVE MOMENT**
>
> Think of a difficult situation you have experienced. It does not have to be the worst thing you have endured, but a time in which you struggled.
>   Write down:
> - What you did at the time of crisis
> - How you learned to adapt
> - What you did well
> - What skills you developed
> - What lessons you learned through the process and how that has/or will guide you moving forward.

Alongside personal reflection, there are many ways to work with – and through – transgenerational and intergenerational trauma. One of the most well-known therapeutic modes is talking therapy, which is what we tend to think of when we hear the term "therapy". This involves seeing a trained mental health professional (this could also be a mental health practitioner, psychologist, mental health coach or counsellor), and addressing any difficulties you may be having with your mental or emotional health.

Therapeutic intervention can often get a bad reputation in our communities because of the many historical, cultural and systemic factors we've already discussed. There is often a deep-rooted mistrust of authorities, a stigma around mental health issues, a lack of diverse and culturally sensitive therapists, and a desire to keep problems "within the family". However, talking therapy can provide a safe and structured space for people to express themselves, gain insight, problem-solve and build coping strategies. There are a wide range of therapies available, so it is worth doing some research to see what suits you best.

> **TOP TIP:** Find the right therapist for you
>
> When choosing a therapist, it's important to consider whether they will be able to support your cultural, religious, ethnic or race-based needs. Do not be afraid to ask them about their background and experience working with people from your community. A great organization to start with is the Black, African and Asian Therapy Network, which lists qualified practitioners from global-majority backgrounds.
>
> To find therapists from the global majority, you can check out the Black, African and Asian Therapy Network: www.baatn.org.uk

Other popular therapies include Mindfulness-Based Stress Reduction (MBSR), as well as Mindfulness-Based Cognitive Therapy. These are therapies that integrate Western therapeutic techniques with Eastern mindfulness approaches.

Mindfulness is the practice of being fully present and aware in the current moment without judgement. Skills learned through mindfulness or mindfulness-based therapies support people to remain in the moment, thus reducing the risk of rumination, self-judgement and overthinking. It can also provide tools for people experiencing flashbacks and intrusive thoughts.

> **TOP TIP: Practise mindful sound-awareness**
>
> This activity will help you cultivate mindfulness by directing your attention to the present moment through your sense of hearing. It will help you tune into your surroundings and can be practised at any time of day or in any location.
> - Close your eyes. If closing your eyes feels uncomfortable, then find a spot in the distance to focus on, or simply lower your gaze.
> - Start to focus your attention on the noises you can hear. Listen without judgement or processing.
> - Start to bring your awareness to the closest sound you can hear in your vicinity. Perhaps it's a clock ticking, your breath or the whir of the radiator.
> - Now, start to broaden your awareness to sounds a little bit further out from where you are. Perhaps it's birds singing outside, your neighbour's dogs barking or the gentle murmur of voices in the next room.

- Finally, extend your consciousness to the furthest sound you can hear. Perhaps it's a train in the distance or an airplane in the sky.
- Sit for a few minutes, allowing your sense of sound to absorb these various noises. Try not to place any judgement or scrutiny on what you hear.
- Your mind will wander, and that is okay – simply notice and bring your mind back to the sounds around you.
- After a few moments, bring your awareness back to the room. Slowly open your eyes, take a few deep breaths and return back to your day.

Support groups and group therapy, either in person or online, can also be useful if you'd like to speak to people who have a similar lived experience. Connecting with others who have a shared understanding can create feelings of inclusion, connection, community and validation. I have delivered many BIPOC-specific wellbeing workshops over the years, and there is something very powerful about being surrounded by others who understand your journey.

Support groups are similar to one-to-one therapeutic support, in that they provide a safe space for participants to share, connect and feel heard. These spaces provide an opportunity for both expert advice and peer-to-peer learning from others who have faced similar struggles. Support groups will often be related to a specific topic. In this context, groups to seek out might be ones that focus on trauma and PTSD, grief and loss, mental health support, caregiver support, addiction recovery, parenting support, disability and chronic illness, culturally specific support groups or domestic violence groups. These are just a few examples of what's available.

> **CASE STUDY:** Support group for parents and carers
>
> During the Covid-19 pandemic, I delivered workshops for parents on supporting the mental health of the children in their care. The parents were from diverse cultural backgrounds, and many were in groups at high risk of impact from Covid-19.
>
> We discussed ways of managing mental health, and tools and techniques for supporting children with theirs. Members of the group shared their experiences, as well as some of the challenges they were facing at the time, e.g., mistrust of authorities, separation from family abroad, little access to green spaces and difficulties with home schooling. The fact that this was a global-majority space meant that attendees felt comfortable to share challenges that were unique to their socio-cultural experiences.

BODY BASED APPROACHES

Alongside talking-based approaches, there are several body-based approaches that can provide support. Our bodies hold the stories of the past, and one way to release stuck and held emotional tension is through physical and energetic movement.

Therapies such as yoga therapy, movement therapy, somatic experiencing and even weight training can help to release stuck bodily patterns, increase body awareness, regulate the nervous system and discharge trapped energy. Many of our indigenous ancestors used music, movement and rhythm as a form of expression and to connect to their higher selves. We can tune into that wisdom to release negative feelings and stored-up emotions.

> **TOP TIP:** Release emotion through movement
>
> Releasing emotions with music and movement can be a powerful way to discharge. Here are some simple steps:
> - Find a time when and a space where you will not be disturbed. To truly access this work, you need to feel safe and comfortable enough to let go.
> - Choose a type of music that resonates with the feelings you wish to release. For example, if I'm feeling sad, I'll usually go with melancholy music, but if it's anger I'm working with, I will choose something with heavy bass and beats.
> - As the music starts to play, allow yourself to tune in to the rhythm, bass and melody. Allow your body to move in whatever way feels natural. You might want to rock, sway, jump, stomp or shout.
> - Continue to stay present, allowing your body to move with the flow and your emotions to run through you. There is no need for typical "dance moves". Whatever you choose to do will be right.
> - When you are ready, gradually slow down your movements and allow your body to sway from side to side before coming to a stationary position.

- Take some time to reflect on your experience. Perhaps you want to journal on what you feel and compare your emotional state to before your movement practice. When you are finished, take time to indulge in some self-care – shower, drink water or do some meditation to slow down and integrate your experience.

Body-based holistic and alternative therapies can also help as a form of maintenance, particularly for issues like chronic stress and anxiety. Energy work is any form of holistic therapy based on the belief that a universal energy flows through all living things. It is not aligned to a particular religion, but this idea can be found in various cultures – it's called *chi* in traditional Chinese medicine, *prana* in yogic philosophy, *ki* in Japanese culture, and *asé* in the Yoruba West African spiritual practices, among countless others across the globe. Energy work aims to balance and improve the flow of energy in the person that is being treated. These techniques may include placing hands on the client, visualization, intention setting or distance healing, wherein a practitioner transfers energy to their client from any distance.

As we have seen, trauma can impact people on a physiological, spiritual and epigenetic level. Energy work can help to release blocked energy, provide a space for relaxation, rejuvenate the body and mind, and provide a space for self-care. When seeking out an energy healer always investigate their qualifications to ensure that they are fully registered and insured. I would also ask them about their experiences of working with trauma to ensure that they are a trauma informed practitioner.

Complementary therapies – acupuncture, reflexology, massage therapy, aromatherapy, nutritional therapy and herbalism, to name a few – recognize the importance of energy and flow, too. These therapies can often help to address the more physical symptoms associated with trauma and stress.

Lifestyle factors also play a big part in the management of trauma and trauma-related conditions. As mentioned earlier, transgenerational trauma can impact individuals on an epigenetic level, leading to risk of ill health. There is mounting evidence to suggest that lifestyle factors, such as diet, physical activity, obesity, tobacco smoking, alcohol consumption, environmental pollutants, psychological stress and working night shifts, may modify epigenetic patterns (Alegría-Torres et al.). This highlights that although genetics do play a role in the development of illness, we do have a good degree of power over our health outcomes.

> **REFLECTIVE MOMENT**
>
> Take some time to reflect on your overall health and wellbeing. Consider these categories one at a time: nutrition, physical activity, drug and alcohol usage, physical environment (home, local area), stress management and sleep. For each one, answer the following questions:
>
> - On a scale of 1–10, how happy am I with this area of my life?
> - What is going well in this area?

- What do I need to improve?
- What are the barriers to stop me from improving this area?
- What is one step I can take to improve this area of my life? What kind of support will I need to get there?

When making lifestyle changes, it is important to take things one step at a time. Pick one or two areas to start with, and once you have established new habits, you can build up from there.

TAMING THE STRESS RESPONSE

Along with everyday lifestyle factors and healing therapies, there are times when we need to manage our trauma responses in the moment. When someone experiences a stressful experience or incident, their body can go into "fight, flight, freeze or fawn", its automatic response to threats or danger. This means that they will automatically try to confront the threat (fight), escape (flight), play dead (freeze) or cooperate with the threat (fawn).

In modern times, our fight response may manifest as you snapping at your loved ones, while flight may be avoiding social situations. Freeze might look like clamming up verbally, and fawn could mean that you befriend someone who is causing you harm.

These responses are part of our primal survival mechanism and help us to keep safe in times of danger. However, trauma can overstimulate these responses, or cause us to have difficulty switching off, which can have long-term effects on various bodily systems, such as the immune and the nervous systems.

> **REFLECTIVE MOMENT**
>
> How does your stress response tend to play out when you feel under threat? Do you fight, flight, freeze or fawn? What can you do to support yourself during those moments of stress?

It is important to recognize that everyone is different, and what works for one person may not work for another – this is why it is important to explore and find out what suits you. It is also important to know that although these solutions provide temporary relief, it is important to pair them with some longer-term solutions for longer lasting healing and trauma recovery.

TOP TIP: Deactivate the stress response

Short-term stress is normal and natural. However, we need to find ways to complete the stress cycle for our body to return to its state of rest as quickly as possible. We can do this by deactivating the stress response. Thankfully, there are several ways to do so.

1. **Deep breathing:** Deep breathing activates the body's relaxation response. Take slow, deep inhales through the nose and exhales through the mouth. Try to make

the exhales longer than the inhales.
2. **Grounding exercises:** Like mindfulness techniques, grounding exercises bring you into the here and now. However, they do so by tuning in to your senses, taking your attention away from distressing thoughts or feelings and bringing you back into the present. Exercises you can try are submerging your hands in water, holding ice, performing light physical activity, listening to your surroundings, listening to music, playing with a stress ball or petting an animal.
3. **Progressive muscle relaxation:** In this exercise, you focus on tensing all your muscles one at a time and then releasing them. This helps to release muscular tension and create a sense of calm. Take a comfortable seat or lay down. Start by taking some deep breaths, and then begin tensing the muscles in your lower body. Tense your toes, then calves, then thighs, etc., and work your way up to your head. Take the movement to a place of tension but not pain, and hold each area for a count of five. Slowly release the muscles after five seconds, and mentally say the word "relax" as you let go.
4. **Laughter:** It is difficult to feel stressed while rolling on the floor laughing. Laughter releases endorphins that directly counteract stress hormones. Watching a funny film, reminiscing on a funny moment or watching YouTube clips of people laughing can get things going.
5. **Orgasm:** This is not the most orthodox approach, but I thought it was worth a mention. Orgasms release feel-good hormones including oxytocin (the love hormone), reduce cortisol (the stress hormone), and can provide deep physical and emotional release.

> **TOP TIP:** Alleviate stress and anxiety with Pranayama
>
> Pranayama is breathwork from the yogic tradition. Try these simple exercises to support stress management and the flow of vital energy around the body,
>
> **Bee breath (Bhramari Pranayama):**
>
> Sit in a comfortable position and close your eyes. Place your thumbs covering your ear canals and your pinkie fingers gently over your eyes. Allow the rest of your fingers to rest on your forehead. This will create a sensation of sensory withdrawal. Take a large inhale and, as you exhale, steadily make a humming/buzzing sound (like the sound of a bee!). Repeat for 10 breaths.
>
> **Deep belly breathing:**
>
> Find a comfortable seat and close your eyes (or lower your eye gaze). Try and keep your shoulders and your posture upright. Place one hand below your belly button and the other on your chest. As you begin to breathe in deeply through your nose, envision your abdomen expanding like a balloon. Notice the hand beneath your belly button as it rises and falls with each exhale, allowing your belly to gradually deflate. Continue for 5–10 minutes. You can also experiment with this practice lying down on the floor for added relaxation.
>
> *Please note that if you have any respiratory conditions, cardiovascular conditions, are pregnant, struggling with severe mental health, are on any medication or have low blood pressure, please consult a medical professional before engaging in breathwork. If you experience any light-headedness during the practice, cease immediately and return to your normal breathing pattern.*

BECOMING AWARE OF YOUR TRIGGERS

An important factor in the healing journey is the recognition of trigger awareness. A trigger is an event, symbol or experience that may activate a stress or trauma response. It can be anything from hearing certain words or sounds, to finding yourself in specific situations, to reaching anniversaries of difficult events, to seeing visual prompts.

I often get asked to speak on panels about mental health in ethnically diverse communities. On occasion, hosts and interviewers will expect me to talk about the stigma of struggling with mental health in our communities while they themselves have horrendously prejudiced views on the topic. This is because they don't know about the systemic barriers that make mental health difficulties a reality in our lived experience as people of colour. When this happens, I can find myself becoming activated, and it can take a toll on my mind and body. I take care to lean on my own healing methods such as moving my body, breathing, journaling or talking things through with my own therapist.

You too can recognize you are feeling triggered if emotional, psychological or physical symptoms start to crop up seemingly out of nowhere. For example, if I am feeling negatively activated, I'll notice my heart rate increasing, my stomach churning, and anxious thoughts running through my head on a loop. Whenever this happens, I know that I need to take some time out to re-centre.

Understanding the mind-body connection is a major part of supporting yourself in the face of triggers. Once you are more aware of your bodily responses, you will start to notice when exactly it happens and how often. As you become more adept at noticing your triggers, you can start to develop coping mechanisms to deal with them. Using your self-care plan from Chapter 1 can help you to find things that soothe you during moments when you feel triggered.

It is useful to know that triggers are not always negative. Positive triggers can bring back or elicit positive emotions. For example, I love cinnamon and eat it all the time. The smell evokes strong memories of warming wintery drinks, the cinnamon doughnuts I used to eat during my childhood, and the warm oats my dad used to make me as a child. Now, whenever I smell cinnamon, I get a warm and fuzzy feeling.

> **REFLECTIVE MOMENT**
>
> Think about a moment in your life when you were really happy. Perhaps it was while doing your favourite hobby or on vacation, or during a live gig. Write down everything you can remember about that event – the smells, the sounds, the emotions you felt and why you enjoyed it so much.
>
> Notice how bringing back those memories makes you feel. Does your body relax into your chair, does a gentle smile creep onto your face?
>
> You can use this exercise any time you want to invoke positive emotions and change your emotional state.

WAYS TO WORK WITH INTERGENERATIONAL WISDOM

We have spoken a lot about intergenerational trauma, but it is important to remember that our communities hold so much intergenerational wisdom. We may have been through many trials and tribulations, but our people are so resilient! When I look back at my own lineage, I feel so proud, and I feel the same way about my global-majority sibling communities, too!

There have been many who came before us who were dedicated to healing, repairing, rebuilding and breaking cultural cycles of trauma. Quite frankly, it is awe-inspiring.

So much of our legacy is focused on the hardships we have endured and the difficulties we still face, but it is important to also bring to focus the wisdom that has been passed on from our ancestors. It has been shown that passing on the lessons from difficult past experiences can foster intergenerational resilience within families.

Intergenerational wisdom is the amalgam of collective knowledge passed down from one generation to another. In can include values, food, music, dance, rituals, cultural traditions, spiritual practices and more. Although much of this wisdom is still present, it can be somewhat disjointed. Some has been lost through the process of colonialization, and some has been co-opted and commodified by global-minority white communities. Think of spiritual practices, such as yoga and meditation, feng shui, Native Indigenous spirituality, Māori culture, and African drumming and dance, which are still present, but have also been appropriated for capital gain in white Western spaces with little benefit to the communities from which they have originated.

We can work toward intergenerational healing by tuning in to that wisdom. Over the past few years, I have been deepening my knowledge of African and Caribbean dance as a form of liberation, and it has been an extremely therapeutic process. I feel more connected to my lineage than ever, and I am empowered to use the tools and practices of my ancestors.

CASE STUDY: Tuning in to intergenerational wisdom

Akmad is a 42-year-old of Filipino descent and first-generation Brit raised in the UK from the age of 7 years old. Akmad had always been a big fan of massage and complementary therapies, but had perceived anything outside of Swedish or sports massages as a bit too "woo-woo".

Akmad attended a wellbeing fair and met a Filipino massage therapist using traditional Filipino and Southeast Asian massage and herbal remedies. Akmad had a treatment with the practitioner and described feeling a deep sense of connection with the techniques used.

Akmad spoke to his mother about his experience and discovered many of the practices he had experienced were part and parcel of his mother's upbringing. He began to research healing modalities across the Asian diaspora and was shocked to find that Western medicine has been influenced by modalities such as traditional Chinese

> medicine, ancient Indian medicine, mindfulness and integrated mind-body care.
>
> Now, whenever Akmad has a medical issue, he approaches it holistically with a respect for both Western medicine and Eastern medicine approaches.

There are so many ways to explore your intergenerational cultural legacy. Some simple ways to get started could be to have conversations with your elders, and share stories and practices with the younger generation. Or, you could research an area of your lineage that you are curious to find out more about – it could be anything from fashion to food to spirituality. It could also be through the arts. After all, most cultures have a rich history of dance, music and performance, and these creative modalities can tell us a lot about the life, history and philosophy of a particular culture.

It can seem overwhelming, but it is a marathon, not a sprint. You can delve in, bit by bit, and take your time. The internet is a wonderful resource, but you may also uncover this wisdom in person, in spaces such as museums, archives, workshops and exhibitions, too.

Tuning into this wisdom not only benefits us as individuals but also future generations. Our stories can help those younger (and older!) than us to navigate meaning, purpose and identity. It also helps us to preserve our culture and the culture of those that came before us. It allows us to fuse ancient knowledge with modern approaches and reinvent what it means to be a member of the global majority, which is key in our journey to transforming transgenerational trauma.

TAKE CARE TAKEAWAYS

- Trauma can impact anyone, but colonial history means secondary and transgenerational trauma can have a particular impact on global-majority communities.
- Trauma can impact us psychologically, emotionally, physically and spiritually.
- Cleaning up your social media feed can provide respite from secondary trauma online.
- Being aware of your triggers and figuring out both short- and long-term healing modalities that work for you are key on the path of trauma recovery.
- Tuning in to intergenerational wisdom is an important part of the healing journey.

AFTERWORD

As you reach the end of the journey, I want to extend my deepest gratitude to you for joining me on this journey of self-exploration.

I know it is not easy to delve into this work. It can be messy, painful, raw and everything in between. I hope you will have found that alongside the darkened shadows, there were also glimmers throughout – glimmers of hope, glimmers of inspiration and glimmers of a new way forward. By the end of this book, I hope you have managed to gain a deeper understanding of yourself, your worth and your place in this world.

This book has been such a pleasure to write. Every step of the way, I have had you, dear reader, as my inspiration and beacon of motivation to keep going. It has been a long process, and when I first began applying to publishers, I got rejection after rejection. The feedback was that the subject matter was not what they were looking for.

I had some mentoring with a well-respected self-help author, who gave me some invaluable feedback on the shape of my project and the sobering (but important) reminder that the literary world is very white, middle-aged and middle class. In other words, most of the editors who would pick up my manuscript would not be able to resonate with my content.

Shortly after that, I had an opportunity to receive funding for book research. The application process was rigorous, and after many written submissions, I was invited by a panel to present the reasons why I believed my research into BIPOC wellbeing was worthy of being funded.

The panel was also all white and middle-aged. I have no awareness of the panel holders' socioeconomic backgrounds, but the language and cultural capital in the room suggested a middle-class demographic. I poured my heart and soul into the interview and tried with all my might to calmly convince the panel that more resources need to be directed toward the BIPOC community.

However, I soon found out that I did not receive the funding, and I was told that a wellbeing resource for people of colour would not necessarily "result in the changes for people of colour that I envisage". I was absolutely devasted and grieved the loss of this funding for a good few days, wallowing in misery and defeatism.

After a few days, I received an anonymous message from someone within the funder's office. They told me that they were sorry I didn't get the funding, that they could assure me that it didn't reflect on my project, and then they encouraged me to apply again.

That was the kick up the bum that I needed. I realized that by reaching out to publishers and funders who were not diverse and not focused on equity and inclusion, I was barking up the wrong tree. I picked myself up, dusted myself off and realigned with my mission. I realized I didn't need funding to research for this book.

AFTERWORD

Working as a BIPOC coach and equality and diversity specialist, and being an expert in the field and a Black woman were enough!

I set up surveys with my clients, compiled my themes and focused on finding a publisher that aligned with my mission – lo and behold, I eventually got there, and here we are!

I tell you this story not to toot my own horn (although I am mighty proud of my work!), but to voice that I, too, have struggled with low self-esteem and a sense of defeat in the face of racial trauma, discrimination and othering. Every single technique outlined in this book has been personally trialled by me in my journey of self-love and self-advocacy. I walk beside you. And through the voyage of this book, I have truly learned to back myself, too.

So, dear reader, as you close these pages, I want to leave you with a gentle reminder that this road does not end here. It has just begun – backing yourself is a lifelong journey and a pathway to self-discovery, improved confidence and cultural joy. There will be ups and downs, so do be gentle with yourself as you learn to ride for yourself.

Remember: you are not alone on this journey. I would love to know what resonated with you the most, and I would love to stay in touch! I invite you to stay connected with me as we continue to support and uplift ourselves and others within our community.

You can find me here:
Instagram: @lildonia.lawrence
Website: www.movewithlildonia.com
LinkedIn: Lildonia Lawrence

BACK YOURSELF

Once again, thank you for allowing me to be part of your wellbeing and cultural reclamation journey. Stay well, keep going and don't forget to BACK YOURSELF!

ACKNOWLEDGEMENTS

I would like to start off by thanking the hundreds of clients who have entrusted me with their experiences and stories. I wouldn't be where I am now if it wasn't for your support. Thank you for your trust in me as your coach.

Deepest gratitude to those who read my work in the early stages and gave me feedback on the book's progression, content and direction. Harpreet, Nicole, Joseph, Mum – Lillie, Joash, Manu, Ruth, Akosua and Kate – thank you!

Writing can be a lonely endeavour, and I would like to extend a special thanks to my writing teacher, Nancy Stevenson, for re-introducing me to my passion for writing during the pandemic and for your support during the process, from conception to publication.

A special shout out to Sista Jendayi Serwah, with whom I attended a phenomenal course in racial justice. Your passion, wisdom and relentless drive for change has inspired me immensely.

With immense gratitude, I would also like to thank Soraya Nair for seeing the value in this project and pushing it forward, and to the team at Trigger Publishing for making it a reality.

I am profoundly grateful to my nearest and dearest for the incredible support on this journey of anti-racism and racial justice. Your love, kindness, backing and allyship has kept me bolstered, anchored and evolving.

Finally, I would like to thank the ancestors – those who came before me. Your resilience, wisdom, grit, determination and sacrifice has paved the path for my journey.

I am eternally grateful and hope I am making you proud.

Thank you.

GLOSSARY

- **Allyship:** support from privileged individuals to marginalized groups in their fight for equality

- **Anti-Blackness:** specific prejudice, discrimination and hostility directed at Black people

- **BIPOC:** acronym for Black, Indigenous and people of colour, highlighting specific marginalized groups

- **Bystander:** an individual who observes an incident, such as discrimination or harassment, without acting

- **Colonization:** domination and exploitation of a region and its people by a foreign power

- **Colourism:** discrimination based on skin tone, often within the same ethnic or racial group

- **Culture:** shared beliefs, values, customs and behaviours of a group or society

- **Decolonization:** the process of deconstructing colonial ideologies and structures in society

- **Diversity:** varied characteristics and attributes within a group

- **Equality:** ensuring everyone has the same rights and opportunities

- **Equity:** providing fair treatment, opportunities and resources that are tailored to individual needs, in order to achieve equal outcomes

- **Ethnicity:** a group's shared cultural traits, language, ancestry and history

- **Global majority:** term recognizing that people of colour make up most of the world's population

- **Global minority:** term recognizing that white people make up a minority of the world's population

- **Inclusion:** creating environments where all individuals feel valued and supported

- **Marginalization:** relegating certain groups to the fringes of society

- **Microaggression:** subtle but impactful discriminatory action or comment

- **Nationality:** legal relationship between an individual and a state, often associated with citizenship

GLOSSARY

- **Oppression:** prolonged and unjust treatment or control of marginalized groups

- **POC:** people of colour – collective term for non-white individuals

- **Prejudice:** preconceived opinions about individuals or groups based on stereotypes

- **Race:** a social construct categorizing people based on physical traits

- **Racism:** systemic discrimination and oppression based on race

- **Social justice:** equal access to resources, opportunities and rights for all

- **Systemic oppression:** entrenched discrimination against and disadvantages for specific groups within societal systems

- **Texturism:** discrimination based on hair texture, particularly against individuals with coarser, kinkier hair

- **Unconscious bias:** implicit attitudes or stereotypes that affect understanding and decisions

- **White privilege:** the unearned advantages and benefits that white individuals receive in society due to their race

ADDITIONAL RESOURCES

MENTAL HEALTH RESOURCES

- **The Black, African and Asian Therapy Network (BAATN)** – baatn.org.uk
A network of therapists providing culturally sensitive psychotherapy and counselling services for Black, African and Asian communities

- **Black Beetle Health** – https://www.blackbeetlehealth.co.uk/
Education and health promotion for LGBTQ+ Black people and people of colour

- **Black Minds Matter UK** – blackmindsmatteruk.com
Free mental health support to Black individuals and families, including therapy sessions with qualified Black therapists

- **Black Learning Achievement and Mental Health (BLAM UK)** – blamcharity.co.uk
Education, advocacy and community empowerment that supports the mental health and wellbeing of Black individuals

- **British Association for Counselling and Psychotherapy (BACP)** – bacp.co.uk
  Directory of qualified therapists, some of whom specialize in working with individuals from diverse backgrounds, including BIPOC communities

- **Mind** – mind.org.uk
  UK mental health charity that has a branch that focuses on providing support and resources for people from Black, Asian and Minority Ethnic communities

- **Nilaari** – nilaari.co.uk
  Culturally appropriate counselling, advocacy and support for individuals from BAME communities in Bristol and the surrounding areas

- **Taraki** – taraki.uk
  Resources, support groups and counselling services tailored to the needs of South Asian communities in the UK

FAITH-SPECIFIC RESOURCES

- **Imaan** – imaan.org.uk
  Support, resources and advocacy for LGBTQ+ Muslims, including mental health support and counselling

- **Jewish Care** – jewishcare.org
  Support services for the Jewish community in the UK, including mental health support, counselling and therapy

ADDITIONAL RESOURCES

- **Muslim Youth Helpline** – myh.org.uk
  Confidential support and advice for young Muslims in the UK, including counselling services for mental health issues

- **Sikh Your Mind** – sikhyourmind.com
  Resources, support groups and culturally sensitive counselling services tailored to the Sikh community

SUPPORT FOR ADDRESSING DISCRIMINATION

- **Equality and Human Rights Commission (EHRC)** – equalityhumanrights.com
  Guidance, resources and support for individuals experiencing discrimination, including racial discrimination, in various areas of life, including work

- **Southall Black Sisters** – southallblacksisters.org.uk
  Advocacy, advice and support for Black and minority ethnic women experiencing gender-based violence, discrimination and other forms of oppression

- **Stonewall** – stonewall.org.uk
  Support and resources for LGBTQ+ individuals, including those from BIPOC backgrounds, facing discrimination and mental health challenges

- **Stop Hate UK** – stophateuk.org
  Support, advice and advocacy services for individuals and communities affected by hate crimes or incidents, working

to raise awareness and promote understanding and tolerance in society

- **Thrive LDN** – thriveldn.co.uk
  Citywide movement to improve the mental health and wellbeing of all Londoners, including initiatives targeted toward addressing racism and discrimination

- **UK Government Equalities Office** – gov.uk/government/organisations/government-equalities-office
  Guidance and resources on addressing discrimination and racism, including support for individuals facing discrimination at work

REFERENCES

Alegría-Torres, J. A., Baccarelli, A., & Bollati, V. (2011). Epigenetics and lifestyle. *Epigenomics*, 3(3), 267-277.

BBC. (10 February 2017). Trump's executive order: Who does travel ban affect? Available at: https://www.bbc.co.uk/news/world-us-canada-38781302

BBC Stories. (26 January 2019). Meet the kids who grew up in Chinese takeaways. Available at: https://www.youtube.com/watch?v=Ii9o8B_9sXo

Beschloss, M. (6 May 2014). How an experiment with dolls helped lead to school integration. *The New York Times*. Available at: https://www.nytimes.com/2014/05/07/upshot/how-an-experiment-with-dolls-helped-lead-to-school-integration.html

Bilkhu, R. K. (23 June 2020). Shaadi.com: Dating site removes skin tone filter after backlash. BBC News. Available at: https://www.bbc.com/news/newsbeat-53146969

Bó, B., Zimmer, Z., & Rada, C. (2020). The Structure and Determinants of Intergenerational Support Exchange Flows in an Eastern European Setting. *Research on Aging*, 42(9-10), 262-271. Available at: https://doi.org/10.1177/0164027520920026

Corra, M. (2020). Inequality and Multiracial Gatekeeping. *Sociological Focus*, 53(3), 293-321. Available at: https://doi.org/10.1080/00380237.2020.1784331

Costs of War Project. (n.d.). Profiling. Watson Institute for International and Public Affairs, Brown University. Available at: https://watson.brown.edu/costsofwar/costs/social/rights/profiling

Craddock, N., Dlova, N., & Diedrichs, P. C. (August 2018). Colourism: a global adolescent health concern. *Current Opinion in Pediatrics*, 30(4), 472-477. https://doi.org/10.1097/MOP.0000000000000638

Curington, C. V., Lundquist, J. H., & Lin, K.H. (2021). *The Dating Divide: Race and Desire in the Era of Online Romance*. University of California Press.

Darwish, R. (4 December 2018). Arabic speakers on Twitter campaign to make "abeed" the new N-word. Al Bawaba. Available at: https://www.albawaba.com/loop/arabic-speakers-twitter-campaign-make-abeed-new-n-word-1221896

Dashorst, P., Mooren, T. M., Kleber, R. J., de Jong, P. J., & Huntjens, R. J. C. (30 August 2019). Intergenerational consequences of the Holocaust on offspring mental health: A systematic review of associated factors and mechanisms. *European Journal of Psychotraumatology*, 10(1). Available at: https://www.ncbi.nlm.nih.gov/pmc/articles/PMC6720013/

DeGruy, J. (2005). *Post Traumatic Slave Syndrome: America's Legacy of Enduring Injury and Healing*. Uptone Press.

Deshpande, M. S. (2010). History of the Indian Caste System and Its Impact on India Today. California Polytechnic State University. Available at: https://digitalcommons.calpoly.edu/cgi/viewcontent.cgi?article=1043&context=socssp

Du Bois, W. E. B. (2009). *The Souls of Black Folk*. Oxford World's Classics.

REFERENCES

Elliott, J. (1970). *Eye of the Storm*. Available at: https://www.youtube.com/watch?v=jSwZQ1AzjOg

Farid, H., Stack-Dunniber, H., Molina, R., Nosal, C., Mendiola, M., & Hacker, M. (2021). Discrimination, Microaggressions, and Perceptions of Institutional Response in an Academic Obstetrics and Gynecology Department. *Cureus*, 13(6). Available at: https://doi.org/10.7759/cureus.15993

FDA. (23 November 2021). Mercury Poisoning Linked to Skin Products. US Food and Drug Administration. Available at: https://www.fda.gov/consumers/consumer-updates/mercury-poisoning-linked-skin-products

Gadermann, A. M., Petteni, M. G., Janus, M., Puyat, J., Guhn, M., & Georgiades, K. (15 February 2022). Prevalence of Mental Health Disorders Among Immigrant, Refugee, and Nonimmigrant Children and Youth in British Columbia, Canada. *JAMA Network Open*, 5(2). Available at: https://doi.org/10.1001/jamanetworkopen.2021.44934

Galloway, J. (26 September 2018). Online dating while black: How racial discrimination affects which way we swipe. *The Tulane Hullabaloo*. Available at: https://tulanehullabaloo.com/43436/intersections/online-dating-while-black/

Glenn, E. N. (February 2008). Yearning for Lightness: Transnational Circuits in the Marketing and Consumption of Skin Lighteners. *Gender & Society*, 22(3), 281-302. Available at: https://www.researchgate.net/publication/249668094_Yearning_for_Lightness_Transnational_Circuits_in_the_Marketing_and_Consumption_of_Skin_Lighteners

Goldsmith, A. H., Hamilton, D., & Darity Jr, W. (2007). From Dark to Light: Skin Color and Wages among African-Americans. *The Journal of Human Resources*, 42(4), 701-738. Retrieved from https://www.jstor.org/stable/40057327

Greenwald, A. G., McGhee, D. E., & Schwartz, J. L. K. (1998). Measuring individual differences in implicit cognition: The implicit association test. *Journal of Personality and Social Psychology*, 74(6), 1464-1480.

Griffin, B., & Hu, W. (June 2019). Parental career expectations: effect on medical students' career attitudes over time. *Medical Education*, 53(6), 584-592. Available at: https://doi.org/10.1111/medu.13812

Hall, R. E. (19 February 2021). Women of color spend more than $8 billion on bleaching creams worldwide every year. The Conversation. Available at: https://theconversation.com/women-of-color-spend-more-than-8-billion-on-bleaching-creams-worldwide-every-year-153178

Hannon, L., DeFina, R., & Bruch, S. (5 September 2013). The Relationship Between Skin Tone and School Suspension for African Americans. *Race and Social Problems*, 5, 281-295. Available at: https://doi.org/10.1007/s12552-013-9104-z

Head, T. (11 June 2021). Interracial Marriage Laws History and Timeline. ThoughtCo. Available at: https://www.thoughtco.com/interracial-marriage-laws-721611

Holman, E. A., Garfin, D. R., & Silver, R. C. (2019). Media Exposure to Collective Trauma, Mental Health, and Functioning: Does It Matter What You See? *Clinical Psychological Science*, 8(1), 111–124. Available at: https://doi.org/10.1177/2167702619858300

Joblist. (21 September 2021). The impact of parental influence - Career Edition. Available at: https://www.joblist.com/trends/the-impact-of-parental-influence-career-edition

Kinouani, G. (19 August 2020). There is racism even in our nurseries and Black children like mine are suffering. *Metro*. Available at: https://metro.co.uk/2020/08/19/children-are-suffering-racism-nursery-cannot-turn-away-13149595/

REFERENCES

Leão, T. S., Sundquist, J., Johansson, L. M., Johansson, S.-E., & Sundquist, K. (19 January 2017). Incidence of Mental Disorders in Second-Generation Immigrants in Sweden: A Four-Year Cohort Study. *Ethnicity & Health*, 10(3), 243-256. Available at: https://doi.org/10.1080/13557850500096878

Mallick, M. (2021, May 20). Marketing Still Has a Colorism Problem. Harvard Business Review. Available at: https://hbr.org/2021/05/marketing-still-has-a-colorism-problem

McTaggart, N., Cox, V., & Heldman, C. (2021). Representations of Black Women in Hollywood. Available at: https://www.nywift.org/wp-content/uploads/2021/12/rep-of-black-women-in-hollywood-report.pdf

Noe-Bustamante, L., Gonzalez-Barrera, A., Edwards, K., Mora, L., & Lopez, M. H. (4 November 2021). Majority of Latinos say skin color impacts opportunity in America and shapes daily life. Pew Research Center. Available at: https://www.pewresearch.org/hispanic/2021/11/04/majority-of-latinos-say-skin-color-impacts-opportunity-in-america-and-shapes-daily-life/

Omi, M., & Winant, H. (1994). *Racial Formation in the United States: From the 1960s to the 1990s*. Routledge.

Oreopoulos, P. (November 2011). Why Do Skilled Immigrants Struggle in the Labor Market? A Field Experiment with Thirteen Thousand Resumes. *American Economic Journal: Economic Policy*, 3(4), 148-171. Available at: https://doi.org/10.1257/pol.3.4.148

Oxford English Dictionary. (n.d.). Colourism. Available at: https://www.oed.com/search/dictionary/?scope=Entries&q=colourism

Rahman, M. (14 December 2020). The Causes, Contributors, and Consequences of Colorism Among Various Cultures.

Available at: https://digitalcommons.wayne.edu/cgi/viewcontent.cgi?article=1069&context=honorstheses

Sarkisian, N., & Gerstel, N. (2008). Till marriage do us part: Adult children's relationships with their parents. *Journal of Marriage and Family*, 70(2), 360-376. Available at: https://doi.org/10.1111/j.1741-3737.2008.00487.x

Stop Hate UK. (n.d.). Stop Hate UK Statistical Review 2021-22. Available at: https://www.stophateuk.org/wp-content/uploads/2022/09/Annual-report-2122-Draft-v2.pdf

Teaching for Change. (n.d.). Overview of the Development of Ethnic, Gender, Disability, and Class Identity and Attitudes in Children and Youth. Available at: https://www.teachingforchange.org/wp-content/uploads/2012/08/ec_overviewofthedevelopment_english.pdf

Unilever. (n.d.). Purpose-led, future-fit: Unilever Annual Report on Form 20-F 2020. Available at: https://www.unilever.com/files/origin/98141a611d1f91a5a0ed387f7aba0846bcc28f56.pdf/Annual-Report-on-form-20-F-2020.pdf

Velez, B. L., Polihronakis, C. J., Watson, L. B., & Cox, R. (2019). Heterosexism, Racism, and the Mental Health of Sexual Minority People of Color. *The Counseling Psychologist*, 47(1), 129-159. Available at: https://doi.org/10.1177/0011000019828309

Viglione, J., Hannon, L., & DeFina, R. (2011, January). The impact of light skin on prison time for black female offenders. *The Social Science Journal*, 48(1), 250-258. https://doi.org/10.1016/j.soscij.2010.08.003

TRIGGERHUB IS ONE OF THE MOST ELITE AND SCIENTIFICALLY PROVEN FORMS OF MENTAL HEALTH INTERVENTION

Trigger Publishing is the leading independent mental health and wellbeing publisher in the UK and US. Our collection of bibliotherapeutic books and the power of lived experience change lives forever. Our courageous authors' lived experiences and the power of their stories are scientifically endorsed by independent federal, state and privately funded research in the US. These stories are intrinsic elements in reducing stigma, making those with poor mental health feel less alone, giving them the privacy they need to heal, ensuring they are guided by the essential steps to kick-start their own journeys to recovery, and providing hope and inspiration when they need it most.

Clinical and scientific research conducted by assistant professor Dr Kristin Kosyluk and her highly acclaimed team in the Department of Mental Health Law & Policy at the University of South Florida (USF), as well as complementary research by her peers across the US, has independently verified the power of lived experience as a core component in achieving mental health prosperity. Their findings categorically confirm lived experience as a leading method in treating those struggling with poor mental health by significantly reducing stigma and the time it takes for them to seek help, self-help or signposting if they are struggling.

Delivered through TriggerHub, our unique online portal and smartphone app, we make our library of bibliotherapeutic titles and other vital resources accessible to individuals and organizations anywhere, at any time and with complete privacy, a crucial element of recovery. As such, TriggerHub is the primary recommendation across the UK and US for the delivery of lived experiences.

At Trigger Publishing and TriggerHub, we proudly lead the way in making the unseen become seen. We are dedicated to humanizing mental health, breaking stigma and challenging outdated societal values to create real action and impact. Find out more about our world-leading work with lived experience and bibliotherapy via triggerhub.com, or by joining us on:

- 🐦 @triggerhub_
- 📘 @triggerhub.org
- 📷 @triggerhub_

Dr Kristin Kosyluk, PhD, is an assistant professor in the Department of Mental Health Law & Policy at USF, a faculty affiliate of the Louis de la Parte Florida Mental Health Institute, and director of the STigma Action Research (STAR) Lab. Find out more about Dr Kristin Kosyluk, her team and their work by visiting:

USF Department of Mental Health Law & Policy:
www.usf.edu/cbcs/mhlp/index.aspx

USF College of Behavioral and Community Sciences:
www.usf.edu/cbcs/index.aspx

STAR Lab: www.usf.edu/cbcs/mhlp/centers/star-lab/

For more information, visit BJ-Super7.com